MW01115954

COIN COLLECTING BIBLE 2025

The Complete Up-to-Date Guide to Master Identification, Valuation, Preservation, and Profitable Collection Strategies for Beginners to Experts

LINCOLN MOLLETT

TABLE OF CONTENT

INTRODUCTION

Why Coin Collecting is More Relevant Than Ever

In an age where digital transactions dominate and cash is increasingly rare, you might wonder why coin collecting—a hobby centered around physical, tangible objects—continues to thrive. The truth is, coin collecting is more relevant now than ever, and its appeal only grows stronger with time. Imagine holding a piece of history in your hands, a coin that has passed through generations, reflecting the culture, politics, and values of its time. Coins are far more than just currency; they are artifacts, preserving stories and moments from the past. In a world where everything seems fleeting, the permanence of coins offers a unique connection to history, making each piece in your collection a treasure trove of stories waiting to be discovered.

But coin collecting isn't just about nostalgia; it's also about security. We live in uncertain economic times, where markets can fluctuate wildly and traditional investments can lose value overnight. Coins, especially those made from precious metals like gold and silver, have consistently proven to be a reliable store of value. For collectors, this means that your hobby isn't just a pastime—it's a financial safeguard. The coins you collect today could very well be the assets that protect your wealth tomorrow, offering a blend of joy and security that's hard to find in other investments.

There's something truly exhilarating about the hunt for that next coin, the thrill of discovery, and the satisfaction of adding a new piece to your collection. Each coin is a gateway to learning—whether it's delving into the historical context of its minting, appreciating the intricacies of its design, or mastering the art of coin grading. This constant pursuit of knowledge keeps your mind engaged, making coin collecting a hobby that's as mentally stimulating as it is enjoyable.

And let's not forget the community. Thanks to online platforms and social media, the world of coin collecting is more connected than ever. You can easily connect with fellow enthusiasts, share insights, trade coins, and learn from experts all around the globe. This sense of camaraderie not only enriches your collecting experience but also opens up new opportunities to discover rare finds and stay on top of market trends. Speaking of the market, interest in collectible coins has been steadily rising. More and more people are recognizing the value of coins not just as collectibles but as smart investments. This growing interest means a broader selection of coins is available, from ancient relics to modern commemoratives, ensuring that there's always something new and exciting to add to your collection.

Perhaps one of the most meaningful aspects of coin collecting is the legacy it allows you to create. Many collectors start young, inspired by coins handed down from parents or grandparents. These collections become more than just a hobby—they become a family tradition, a legacy that bridges generations. In a world where so much is temporary, passing down a coin collection is a way to share your passion and knowledge with the next generation, ensuring that the history and significance of these coins are appreciated for years to come.

So, why is coin collecting more relevant than ever? Because it's more than just a hobby—it's a journey through history, a way to safeguard your wealth, a pursuit of knowledge, and a connection to a vibrant community. It's a hobby that offers joy, enrichment, and a lasting legacy, making it an incredibly rewarding pursuit in today's fast-paced, ever-changing world. Whether you're just starting out or have been collecting for years, there's never been a better time to dive into the fascinating world of coins.

How Coin Collecting Can Be Both a Passion and a Profitable Investment

Investing has always been a key interest of mine, though I've never been one to follow the conventional paths of stocks and bonds. Living in the U.S. and nurturing a deep appreciation for coins, I've naturally gravitated toward less traditional, yet profoundly rewarding avenues. Coin collecting, in particular, has emerged as a cornerstone of my investment strategy—offering both tangible value and a connection to history that few other assets can provide.

Coins represent more than just a store of wealth; they are, quite literally, pieces of history that can be held in your hand. Each coin in my collection, whether from the U.S. or from distant corners of the world, carries a unique narrative, a story that goes beyond its monetary value. This dual nature of coins, blending historical significance with investment potential, makes them an incredibly compelling asset. My approach is methodical and informed, always guided by a deep understanding of the historical context in which these coins were minted. Whether through online auctions or private collectors, every acquisition is a calculated move in a larger, carefully considered strategy.

The history of U.S. coinage is particularly rich, offering insights into the nation's evolution over the centuries. Understanding the transition from early colonial coins to the official productions of the U.S. Mint is not just fascinating—it's essential for any serious collector. This historical knowledge underpins every decision I make, allowing me to assess the true value of each coin, not just in terms of its market price, but in its broader cultural and historical context.

Over the years, I've developed a rigorous methodology for evaluating coins, relying on a range of specialized resources and tools that provide critical insights into everything from metal content to rarity. This disciplined approach ensures that my collection is not just a hobby, but a well-structured investment portfolio. Platforms like eBay serve as valuable resources for tracking market trends and verifying the current value of my coins, offering a real-time snapshot that is essential for informed decision-making.

But beyond the strategic and financial aspects, coin collecting is a profound passion of mine. It's about more than just accumulating coins—it's about uncovering the stories that each coin carries. Take, for instance, the 1858 U.S. half dollar in my collection. This coin is not merely a piece of silver; it's a tangible relic from a pivotal period in American history, a time when the nation was on the brink of civil war. Coins like these are more than investments—they are connections to the past, offering insights into the events and decisions that shaped our world.

One particularly intriguing aspect of coin collecting is the discovery of error coins—those rare anomalies that escape the minting process with unique imperfections. These coins, like the 1955 doubled die cent, are highly sought after by collectors and investors alike. The existence of such coins adds a layer of excitement and unpredictability to the collection process, transforming it into a pursuit of discovery as much as an investment strategy.

Looking to the future, I am confident in the enduring value of my collection. Coins have a permanence that few other assets can claim. They have been a reliable store of value for thousands of years, and I have no doubt they will continue to be so for many years to come. My intention is to pass this collection down to my children, ensuring that it serves not only as a valuable financial asset but also as a legacy of knowledge, history, and passion.

In an era where digital currencies and virtual assets are becoming increasingly prevalent, the tangible nature of coins stands out. As we move further into the digital age, I believe that physical coins will become even more valuable, cherished not only for their historical and artistic significance but also for their rarity in an increasingly intangible world. This makes them not just a sound financial investment, but a cultural one as well.

As a professional, I approach coin collecting with the same rigor and strategic thinking that one might apply to any serious investment portfolio. It's about making informed decisions, understanding the market, and, most importantly, recognizing the intrinsic value of each coin beyond its face value. This approach not only ensures the growth and preservation of my collection's value but also guarantees that it will continue to be a source of pride and financial security for generations to come. Coin collecting, in this light, is both a passion and a profoundly profitable investment—one that I am confident will continue to yield rewards for years to come.

PART I: THE WORLD OF COIN COLLECTING

CHAPTER 1

Understanding the Coin Market

The coin market is a dynamic and ever-evolving space, shaped by a variety of factors that influence the value and desirability of coins. In this chapter, we will explore the current trends that are defining the market, the historical evolution of numismatic coins, and why collectible coins are increasingly seen as a reliable and profitable investment.

Current Trends and Future Predictions in the Coin Market

In recent years, the coin market has seen a significant shift in the way collectors and investors engage with numismatic coins. One of the most prominent trends is the growing demand for rare and collectible coins as alternative investments. As global financial markets experience fluctuations, many investors are seeking out tangible assets like coins to diversify their portfolios and protect their wealth. This trend has led to a surge in the value of high-quality numismatic coins, particularly those with historical significance or ties to important events.

The rise of online marketplaces has also transformed the coin market, providing collectors and investors with unprecedented access to a global audience. This digital shift has made it easier to buy, sell, and trade coins, increasing market transparency and competitiveness. As we look to the future, the integration of technology, such as blockchain for authentication, is expected to further revolutionize the market, enhancing security and trust for all participants.

The Evolution of Numismatic Coins: A Historical Perspective

Numismatic coins have a rich history that dates back thousands of years, serving not only as a medium of exchange but also as powerful symbols of culture, politics, and art. The first coins, minted in ancient Lydia around 600 BCE, marked the beginning of a new era in trade and commerce. Over the centuries, the designs and functions of coins have evolved, reflecting the changing priorities and values of the societies that produced them.

Throughout history, coins have been used to convey messages of power and authority. For example, Roman coins often featured images of emperors and significant events, serving as propaganda tools to reinforce the ruler's legitimacy and communicate important cultural and political messages. In more recent times, commemorative coins have been issued to celebrate milestones, honor historical figures, and highlight significant cultural achievements.

This historical evolution not only enhances the appeal of numismatic coins but also provides valuable context for collectors. By understanding the historical significance of the coins in their collections, collectors can gain deeper insights into the cultural and political forces that shaped their creation.

Why Collectible Coins Are Increasingly Seen as a Sound Investment

Collectible coins have always held a certain allure, but in today's economic climate, they are increasingly recognized as a sound investment. Unlike traditional investments that can be volatile and subject to market fluctuations, collectible coins offer a level of stability and intrinsic value that is hard to match. Coins made from precious metals like gold and silver have long been considered a safe haven in times of economic uncertainty, but numismatic coins offer even more—historical and cultural value that can appreciate over time.

Investors are drawn to numismatic coins for their rarity, historical significance, and potential for long-term growth. As more people look to diversify their investment portfolios, the demand for high-quality collectible coins continues to rise. This demand, coupled with the limited supply of certain coins, drives up their value, making them a lucrative investment option.

Moreover, the aesthetic and historical appeal of collectible coins adds an additional layer of value. Collectors are often willing to pay a premium for coins that are not only rare but also beautifully designed and well-preserved. As a result, the market for collectible coins is robust, with strong growth prospects for the future.

In this chapter, we have explored the current trends shaping the coin market, the historical evolution of numismatic coins, and the reasons why collectible coins are increasingly seen as a sound investment. Understanding these factors is essential for anyone looking to navigate the coin market successfully, whether as a collector, investor, or both. As we continue to explore the world of coins, we will delve deeper into the strategies and insights that can help you build a valuable and rewarding collection.

CHAPTER 2

Navigating the Types of Coins

The world of coin collecting is vast and varied, with a wide range of coin types that can appeal to different interests and investment goals. Understanding the different types of coins is essential for collectors and investors alike, as it helps in making informed decisions about what to collect, how to assess value, and where to focus efforts.

Numismatic Coins vs. Bullion for Investment

Numismatic coins and bullion are both popular choices for those looking to invest in precious metals, but they come with different characteristics and considerations that are important to understand before making an informed investment decision.

Numismatic coins are collectible coins valued for more than just their metal content; they hold historical, cultural, and aesthetic significance. These coins are often rare, with limited mintages, and are prized for their unique designs and historical importance. The value of numismatic coins is influenced by factors such as rarity, condition, historical demand, and collector interest.

Investing in numismatic coins offers several potential advantages. They possess a strong historical and aesthetic appeal, making them particularly attractive to collectors and enthusiasts. Numismatic coins can also potentially offer high returns, especially if you acquire rare pieces that increase in demand over time. Additionally, they provide diversification benefits, as their value is not solely dependent on the market price of precious metals.

Bullion, on the other hand, refers to investment-grade precious metals in the form of bars or coins with a high metal content. The value of bullion is primarily based on the current market price of the underlying metal, such as gold, silver, platinum, or palladium. Factors like purity, weight, and global demand directly impact the value of bullion.

Investing in bullion offers its own set of benefits. The value of bullion is closely tied to the market price of precious metals, making it a potential hedge against inflation and economic uncertainties. Bullion typically has lower premiums and higher liquidity compared to numismatic coins, making it easier to buy, sell, or trade. It is also considered a safer investment option, as its value is directly linked to the intrinsic worth of the metal content.

When comparing numismatic coins and bullion for investment purposes, several factors should be considered. Price stability is one key factor, as the value of numismatic coins can fluctuate based on collector demand, while bullion's value is more directly influenced by market prices. Profit potential is another consideration, with numismatic coins offering the possibility of high returns over time, but potentially requiring a longer holding period, whereas bullion provides more immediate liquidity. The risks and liquidity associated with each option also vary, with numismatic coins generally carrying higher risks and lower liquidity compared to bullion. However, numismatic coins offer the added advantage of collectibility and aesthetic appeal for those interested in preserving and appreciating historical artifacts.

By thoroughly evaluating the features and advantages of both numismatic coins and bullion, investors can make well-informed decisions that suit their investment objectives, risk appetite, and the prevailing market conditions.

Top Coins for Investors and Collectors Across the Globe

When it comes to the top coins for investors and collectors in 2024, several standout options offer a blend of historical significance, rarity, and potential for appreciation. Here are some of the most notable coins to consider:

1. American Gold Eagle (2024 Edition)

The American Gold Eagle remains a cornerstone for both investors and collectors. The 2024 release, featuring the updated "**Type 2**" design, continues to be a popular choice. Its blend of aesthetic appeal and guaranteed gold content makes it a reliable store of value, particularly in times of economic uncertainty.

2. British Gold Britannia

Another strong contender, the British Gold Britannia, is celebrated for its detailed design and high gold content. The 2024 edition continues this tradition, offering a combination of historical prestige and investment-grade quality. It's a favorite among collectors who appreciate both its beauty and its potential for long-term value appreciation.

3. Franklin Half Dollar (MS-66 or Higher)

For those interested in numismatic coins, the Franklin Half Dollar in mint state MS-66 or higher is a smart investment. Minted between 1948 and 1963, these coins are highly sought after for their rarity in high grades and their connection to mid-20th-century American history. The scarcity and condition of these coins drive their value, making them a solid choice for collectors looking for long-term appreciation.

4. Scarce-Date Morgan Silver Dollars

Morgan Silver Dollars, especially those with scarce dates and mint marks like the 1893-S or 1889-CC, are prized by collectors. These coins combine historical significance with rarity, making them attractive investments. As demand continues to grow, particularly for well-preserved examples, these coins are expected to appreciate further.

5. Platinum American Eagle

For those looking to diversify beyond gold and silver, the Platinum American Eagle is a top pick. First introduced in 1997, this coin is valued not only for its platinum content but also for its role in portfolios seeking exposure to less common precious metals. Its scarcity relative to gold and silver coins makes it a unique addition to any collection.

6. Canadian Palladium Maple Leaf

Palladium coins, like the Canadian Palladium Maple Leaf, offer a compelling investment opportunity. Palladium's rarity and its critical role in industrial applications, particularly in automotive catalytic converters, have driven demand. The Maple Leaf is one of the few palladium coins backed by a government, adding an extra layer of security for investors.

These coins represent a diverse array of investment opportunities, each with its own unique appeal and potential for growth. Whether you're focused on historical value, metal content, or rarity, these selections offer something for every serious collector or investor in 2025.

Most Sought-After Coins in North America, Europe, and Beyond

The most sought-after coins in North America, Europe, and beyond reflect a blend of historical significance, rarity, and cultural value that appeals to both collectors and investors alike. Here's an up-to-date overview of some of the most coveted coins across these regions:

North America

1. 1933 Saint-Gaudens Double Eagle

Often regarded as the most valuable U.S. coin, the 1933 Double Eagle holds legendary status among collectors. With only a handful legally available to private collectors, this coin represents a pinnacle of American numismatics, selling for over $18 million at auction

2. 1794 Flowing Hair Dollar

As the first dollar coin issued by the U.S. government, the 1794 Flowing Hair Dollar is highly prized for its historical significance and rarity. The finest known example sold for over $10 million, making it one of the most expensive coins in the world.

3. Morgan Silver Dollars

Particularly those with scarce dates like the 1893-S or 1889-CC, Morgan Silver Dollars remain favorites among collectors. Their combination of historical importance and scarcity drives continual demand, with well-preserved examples fetching high prices.

Europe

4. 1787 Brasher Doubloon

This gold coin, produced by Ephraim Brasher in the United States but heavily tied to early American and European trading, is extremely rare and highly valued. A Brasher Doubloon recently sold for nearly $10 million, showcasing its immense value.

5. Edward III Florin (England)

Known as the "**Double Leopard**," the Edward III Florin from 1344 is one of the rarest and most valuable coins in Europe, with only three known examples. This coin embodies medieval England's history and is a prized artifact for collectors.

Beyond North America and Europe

6. Chinese Panda Gold Coins

 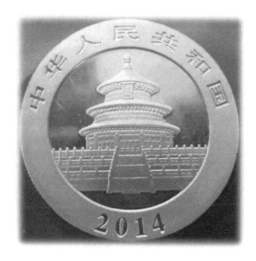

These coins are immensely popular not only for their gold content but also for their annually changing designs, which feature China's beloved giant panda. The Chinese market's growing interest in collectible coins has driven up the demand and value of these issues.

7. Australian Kangaroo Gold Coins

These coins are a staple of the Australian bullion market but also hold appeal for collectors due to their iconic kangaroo design, which changes annually. The combination of high gold content and artistic merit makes them a favorite both in Australia and internationally.

These coins represent some of the most sought-after pieces globally, driven by their rich history, rarity, and the cultural narratives they embody. Whether you are a seasoned collector or an investor, these coins offer both a tangible connection to history and potential financial rewards.

PART II: BUILDING AND VALUING YOUR COLLECTION

CHAPTER 3

Identifying Valuable Coins

Understanding Coin Anatomy and Terminology

Before starting a coin collection, it's essential to familiarize yourself with the basic terminology related to the various parts of a coin. Understanding these terms will help you better appreciate the details and craftsmanship of each coin and make informed decisions as you build your collection.

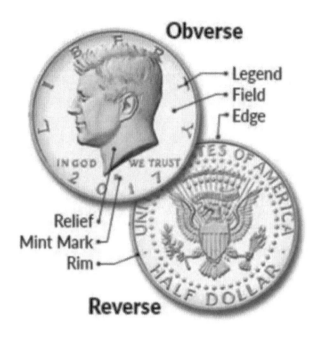

Parts of a Coin

- **Edge:** The edge is the third side of a coin, which can be reeded (with ridges), ornamented, or plain.

- **Field:** The field refers to the flat area of the coin that has no design, providing a background for the coin's raised elements.

- **Mint Mark**: A mint mark consists of letters stamped onto a coin to indicate the mint where it was produced. Current U.S. mints include Philadelphia (P), Denver (D), San Francisco (S), and West Point (W). Historically, other mints such as New Orleans (O), Carson City (CC), Dahlonega (D), and Charlotte (C) also contributed, primarily minting specific types of coins.

- **Motto:** This term refers to any inscription or phrase found on a coin.

- **Obverse**: The obverse is commonly known as the "heads" side of the coin.

- **Relief:** Relief describes the part of the coin's design that is raised above the surface level.

- **Reverse:** The reverse is the opposite side of the obverse, typically referred to as the "tails" side of the coin.

- **Rim:** The rim is the raised edge found around the obverse and reverse sides of a coin, helping to protect the design.

Mint Marks and Their Evolution

Mint marks are used to signify the location where a coin was struck. Initially, the Philadelphia Mint, established in 1792, was the sole U.S. mint, eliminating the need for mint marks until additional mints began operating in 1838. Over time, mint marks became essential identifiers, especially with the opening of mints like New Orleans, Dahlonega, and Charlotte. Notably, Philadelphia coins didn't feature a mint mark until 1942, and it wasn't until the 1979 Susan B. Anthony dollar that the "P" mark was consistently used, except on pennies.

Coin Finishes Explained

Brilliant Uncirculated (BU): This is the most prevalent finish, often found on coins intended for circulation. Despite the wear, coins are only categorized as BU if they retain their original, unused finish.

Proof and Reverse Proof (PR and REV PR)

Proof coins, typically made for collectors, are struck using polished dies, resulting in a mirror-like field with a frosted design. In contrast, reverse proof coins have a frosted field and a mirror-like design, making them rarer due to limited minting.

Burnished Coins

Burnished coins are recognized by their matte, satin finish, achieved by polishing the planchet before striking. These coins often display the West Point (W) mint mark, distinguishing them from traditional bullion coins, which lack a mint mark.

Glossary of Common Numismatic Terms

- **Alloy:** A substance made up of two or more metals combined together.
- **American Numismatic Association (ANA):** A nonprofit organization dedicated to the study and hobby of coin collecting, also known as numismatics.
- **ANACS:** Stands for American Numismatic Association Certification Service, a body that certifies coins.
- **Annealing:** The process of heating blanks (planchets) to relieve or prevent internal stress within the metal.
- **Assay:** The analysis conducted to determine the purity of a metal.
- **Bag Marks**: Small marks or abrasions on a coin caused by contact with other coins within a mint bag.
- **Blank**: The blank piece of metal that is stamped to create a coin; also referred to as a planchet.
- **Bullion**: Precious metals in the form of ingots, coins, or other items that are traded based on their intrinsic metal value.
- **Business Strike**: Coins struck specifically for general circulation, as opposed to proof coins which are made for collectors.
- **CAC (Certified Acceptance Corporation):** A service that verifies the quality of coins that have been previously graded.
- **Cameo (CAM):** A proof or proof-like coin with a distinct contrast between the mirror-like fields and frosty design elements.
- **Circulated:** A term describing a coin that has been used in general circulation and exhibits wear.
- **Clad**: A term used to describe modern "sandwich" coins made from layers of copper and nickel.
- **Commemorative:** A special coin or medal issued to honor a notable person, place, or event.
- **Condition**: Refers to the state of preservation of a coin or numismatic item.
- **Counterfeit:** A fake coin that is not genuine.

- **Denomination:** The monetary value assigned to a specific coin.
- **Designer:** The artist who creates the design for a coin but does not necessarily engrave it.
- **Device:** Any specific design element on a coin.
- **Die:** An engraved tool used to stamp a design into a blank piece of metal to create a coin.
- **Edge:** The third side of a coin, which may be reeded, plain, or ornamented.
- **Engraver:** The person responsible for creating the design or punches used to craft a coin.
- **Error:** A coin that was improperly produced and overlooked during quality control, later released into circulation.
- **Field:** The flat or slightly curved area of a coin that does not contain any design elements.
- **First Strike:** Refers to a coin struck early in the life of a die, often prized for its detail and sharpness.
- **Grade:** A rating indicating the extent of wear on a coin due to circulation.
- **High Relief:** Coins with deep, concave fields due to their design, giving a more three-dimensional appearance.
- **Hub:** A minting tool made of steel, used to create dies.
- **Incuse:** The opposite of relief; the design elements are pressed into the surface of the coin rather than raised.
- **Intrinsic Value (Bullion Value):** The current market value of the precious metal contained within a coin.
- **Legal Tender:** Currency issued by a government that must be accepted as payment for goods and services.
- **Legend:** Any phrase or inscription that appears on a coin.
- **Mint:** A facility where coins are manufactured under government authority.
- **Mint Mark:** Letters stamped onto a coin to indicate the mint where it was produced.
- **Mint Set:** A complete set of coins of each denomination produced by a particular mint.
- **Motto:** An inscription on a coin, often conveying a national or philosophical sentiment.
- **NGC (Numismatic Guaranty Corporation):** A leading coin grading service.
- **Numismatics:** The study and collecting of coins, paper money, and related items used as currency.
- **Obverse:** The front or "heads" side of a coin.

- **PCGS (Professional Coin Grading Service):** Another leading coin grading service.
- **Planchet**: The unmarked metal disc onto which a coin's design is imprinted.
- **Plated**: Describes a coin that has had a thin layer of metal added to its surface.
- **Proof**: A coin that is carefully produced using polished blanks and dies, often struck multiple times for enhanced detail, specifically intended for collectors.
- **Relief**: The part of the coin's design that is elevated above the background surface, as opposed to being recessed.
- **Reverse**: The back side of the coin, commonly referred to as the "tails" side.
- **Rim:** The raised edge around the perimeter of a coin's obverse and reverse, providing protection to the design.
- **Series:** A particular design or motif used consistently over a period of time.
- **Set:** A collection of coins from a series, often including all denominations or variations.
- **Slab:** The plastic holder in which a grading service encapsulates and seals a graded coin.
- **Strike:** The process of stamping a design onto a blank coin planchet.
- **Toning:** The natural coloring that forms on the surface of a coin over time due to the interaction of the metal with external elements.
- **Type:** A category of coins sharing a particular standard design, often produced over a series of years.
- **Uncirculated:** A coin that has never been in general circulation and shows no wear.
- **Variety:** A minor variation from the basic design of a coin, often resulting from changes in dies or minting processes.

The Collector's Mindset: Balancing Passion with Investment

Balancing passion with investment is a delicate art, one that every collector must navigate as they build and curate their collection. For those who begin collecting purely out of passion, the idea of viewing their treasured items through the lens of financial value can seem almost sacrilegious. The emotional attachment to each piece—the stories, the history, and the personal satisfaction they bring—often outweighs any monetary consideration.

However, as time goes on, many collectors find that their instincts as investors naturally begin to develop. This evolution is not about losing the love for collecting, but rather about maturing into a more balanced approach that integrates both passion and prudence. It's about recognizing that while each piece in a collection may hold deep personal significance, it can also represent a smart financial investment that could yield substantial returns in the future.

A seasoned collector understands that the true joy of collecting comes from the process—the thrill of the hunt, the satisfaction of finding a rare item, and the pride in building a collection piece by piece. This passion is what drives collectors to immerse themselves in their chosen field, to study every detail, and to seek out those unique items that resonate with them on a personal level. Yet, as their collection grows, so too does the awareness of its value, both culturally and financially.

Turning a hobby into an investment requires a thoughtful approach. It starts with understanding the market, knowing how to source items, and being able to accurately assess their worth. Preservation is equally crucial; a well-maintained collection not only retains its value but often appreciates over time. Collectors must also be diligent in obtaining authentication and provenance for their items, ensuring that their collection holds up under scrutiny from both historical and market perspectives.

The balance between passion and investment is also evident in the choices collectors make about what to collect. While traditional categories like paintings, sculptures, stamps, and coins remain popular, many collectors are drawn to more eclectic or niche items. These can often be the most valuable, not just in financial terms but in the unique pleasure they bring to the collector. Quirky or unusual collectibles might not always have a ready market, but their rarity and the stories they carry can make them invaluable.

The key is to follow your passion first and foremost. Collect because you love it, because the act of collecting brings you joy and fulfillment. If you do so, the investment aspect often follows naturally. A well-curated collection, built on genuine interest and knowledge, is more likely to appreciate in value, providing financial benefits alongside the personal satisfaction it offers.

Collectors must also be aware of the broader market and any legal or logistical challenges they might face. For instance, restrictions on the movement of certain artifacts can limit a collector's ability to sell their items abroad, as seen with laws like the Antiquities and Art Treasures Act. Being informed about such regulations and planning accordingly is part of the responsibility that comes with managing a valuable collection.

Ultimately, the true return for a passionate collector is not just the financial gain, but the happiness and fulfillment derived from building a collection with care and dedication. The value of a collection is not just in its potential for profit, but in the personal journey it represents—a journey where passion and investment are not mutually exclusive, but rather, complementary forces that together create something truly special.

Key Factors in Determining a Coin's Value

When it comes to determining the value of a coin, there are several key factors that collectors and investors need to consider. While it's tempting to assume that the age of a coin is the most important determinant of its value, the reality is far more complex. The value of a coin is primarily driven by three critical variables: **mintage number**, **condition (or grade),** and **market demand**.

First and foremost is the **mintage number**—the quantity of coins produced in a particular year and at a specific mint. Not every coin is minted in equal numbers; some years see high production runs, while others produce significantly fewer coins. A coin with a lower mintage number is generally rarer, and rarity often translates to higher value. For example, a coin minted in a year when production was limited will typically be more valuable than a coin from a year with a large mintage, even if the coins are otherwise identical. This rarity makes low-mintage coins particularly attractive to collectors who seek out scarce items to enhance their collections.

Next, the **condition or grade** of a coin is crucial in determining its value. Coins are graded based on their state of preservation, with higher grades indicating better condition. A coin that has been well-preserved and shows little to no signs of wear will command a higher price than one that has been circulated and shows significant wear and tear. The grading process is detailed and nuanced, often involving professional evaluation to assign a numerical grade that reflects the coin's condition. Coins in pristine condition can be exponentially more valuable than their lower-grade counterparts, even if they are otherwise the same in terms of mintage and design.

Lastly, **demand** plays a significant role in a coin's value. Some coins are perpetually popular among collectors, consistently fetching high prices regardless of their mintage or grade. For instance, Morgan Silver Dollars are always in high demand, making them a staple at coin shows and auctions. On the other hand, some coins, like Peace Dollars, may not generate as much interest, even if they share similar characteristics with more popular coins. Additionally, some coins experience cyclical demand, where their popularity—and thus their value—rises and falls over time. Buffalo nickels and Mercury dimes are examples of coins that go through these cycles of fluctuating demand.

In summary, the value of a coin is determined by a combination of its mintage number, condition, and market demand. While these factors are all crucial, it's important to remember that the collector's market can be unpredictable. A coin that is less sought after today may become highly desirable in the future, and vice versa. Therefore, understanding these variables and keeping an eye on market trends is essential for anyone looking to buy, sell, or invest in coins.

Global Coin Grading Standards and What They Mean for You

Grading coins is an intricate process that combines both art and science, requiring a deep understanding of various factors that contribute to a coin's overall condition. The process involves assigning a grade to a coin based on established standards recognized by the numismatic community. Key factors such as the strength of the strike, the level of wear, the presence of contact marks, and the overall visual appeal of the coin all play a role in determining its grade. This grade is typically expressed as a number on a scale from 1 to 70, with a grade of 70 representing a perfect, flawless coin. This scale, known as the **Sheldon Grading Scale**, has become the industry standard for coin grading.

While many collectors can learn to grade coins with a reasonable degree of accuracy through practice and experience, achieving the precision required for professional grading is a skill few can master. The condition of a coin is a critical determinant of its value, and even minor, easily overlooked imperfections can significantly impact a coin's worth. Coins that have been carefully preserved and remain in their original, uncirculated condition are classified as "mint state" coins. Those that have seen minimal circulation but still retain a near-new appearance are often graded as "about uncirculated."

The most respected third-party grading services in the numismatic world are the **Numismatic Guaranty Corporation (NGC)** and the **Professional Coin Grading Service (PCGS).** Before assigning a grade, these organizations first authenticate each coin to ensure it has not been cleaned, altered, or tampered with. The grading process itself is rigorous, involving at least two highly trained graders who examine each coin to ensure an accurate and consistent assessment.

NGC WEBSITE

PCGS WEBSITE

Opting for professional grading offers several benefits:

- ❖ **Peace of Mind**: Professional grading provides assurance that your coin is authentic and has been certified as genuine.

- ❖ **Expert Grading**: Coins are evaluated by experts who assign a precise numerical grade reflecting the coin's condition.

- ❖ **Global Recognition**: Coins graded by NGC or PCGS are universally recognized and accepted by dealers and collectors worldwide.

- ❖ **Protection and Preservation**: After grading, each coin is sealed in an archival acrylic holder, preserving its condition and confirming its authenticity permanently.

- ❖ **Additional Pedigrees**: In some cases, coins may receive additional certifications or pedigrees, such as "first strike" or "hoard finds," which are noted on the grading label.

- ❖ **Unique Registration**: Each graded coin is assigned a unique registration number, allowing collectors to verify their coin's details online.

Understanding The Sheldon Coin Grading Scale

The Sheldon Grading Scale, developed by Dr. William H. Sheldon in 1949, is the foundation of modern coin grading. This 70-point scale was originally designed to assess large cents, but it has since been adopted universally across all coin types. The scale ranges from a grade of "1," indicating a coin that is barely recognizable with significant damage, to "70," which signifies a coin that is flawless even under five times magnification. The Sheldon Scale is employed by major grading services such as NGC and PCGS, and it forms the basis for the grading standards set by the American Numismatic Association (ANA).

In essence, coin grading is a meticulous process that significantly influences the market value of a coin. The combination of authentication, precise grading, and proper preservation ensures that collectors and investors alike can trust the value assigned to their coins. Whether you are a novice or an experienced collector, understanding the intricacies of coin grading is essential to building a valuable and respected collection.

Business Strike – Coins produced primarily for circulation and intended for everyday use in commerce, rather than being created specifically for collectors.

Proof – Typically crafted for collectors, not for general circulation. These coins are characterized by their exceptional detail and often exhibit a brilliant, mirror-like finish. The term "Proof" refers to the special method of production, rather than the coin's grade, and usually suggests a superior condition unless otherwise specified.

Mint State – The terms Mint State (MS) and Uncirculated (Unc.) are used interchangeably to describe coins that show no signs of wear. However, coins in this category can exhibit slight variations due to minor surface imperfections, which are categorized as follows:

❖ **Perfect Uncirculated (MS-70)** – Coins in this condition are in perfect, new condition with no signs of wear. They represent the highest quality possible, with no scratches, handling marks, or contact with other coins. Very few circulation-issue coins are found in this pristine condition.

❖ **Gem Uncirculated (MS-65)** – These coins are in above-average uncirculated condition, typically exhibiting a brilliant luster or slight toning, with minimal contact marks on the surface or edges.

❖ **Choice Uncirculated (MS-63)** – Coins that may have some noticeable contact marks or blemishes in key areas. The luster may be somewhat impaired.

❖ **Uncirculated (MS-60)** – A coin that shows no trace of wear but may have several contact marks and a surface that could be spotted or lack luster.

❖ **Choice About Uncirculated (AU-55)** – Shows slight friction on the high points of the design, with most of the original mint luster remaining.

❖ **About Uncirculated (AU-50)** – Displays light wear on many of the high points, with at least half of the mint luster still visible.

❖ **Choice Extremely Fine (EF-45)** – Exhibits light overall wear on the highest points, with all design details remaining sharp. Some mint luster may still be present.

❖ **Extremely Fine (EF-40)** – Light wear is evident throughout the design, but all features are sharp and well-defined. Traces of luster may be visible.

❖ **Choice Very Fine (VF-30)** – Light, even wear across the surface and highest parts of the design, with sharp lettering and major features.

❖ **Very Fine (VF-20)** – Moderate wear on the high points of the design, with all major details clearly defined.

❖ **Fine (F-12)** – Moderate to considerable even wear, with the entire design remaining bold and the coin maintaining a generally pleasing appearance.

❖ **Very Good (VG-8)** – Well-worn, with the main features still clear and bold, though somewhat flattened.

❖ **Good (G-4)** – Heavily worn, with the design visible but faint in places. Many details appear flat.

❖ **About Good (AG-3)** – Extremely worn down, with sections of the lettering, date, and legend nearly smoothed out, making the date difficult to decipher.

CHAPTER 4

Mastering the Coin Market

Proven Strategies for Profitable Coin Collecting

Every coin collector takes pride in their collection, and rightfully so. The journey of building a unique and valuable collection, however, requires more than just passion; it requires a strategic approach. While experience is crucial, it's just one part of the equation. To excel as a coin collector, there are several key strategies you should follow, each designed to ensure that you not only enjoy your hobby but also stay motivated and make informed decisions along the way.

Develop a Strategic Approach from the Start

The foundation of a successful coin collection begins with a well-thought-out plan. Collecting coins isn't just about amassing as many pieces as possible; it's about curating a collection that is unique and reflective of your interests. This requires setting clear goals, focusing on specific categories or themes, and avoiding impulsive decisions that could lead to a disorganized or less valuable collection.

Specialize to Stand Out

One of the most effective strategies in coin collecting is specialization. By focusing on a particular category—whether it's historic coins, error coins, proof coins, bullion coins, or those commemorating specific events—you can build a collection that is both unique and valuable. Specializing allows you to develop deep knowledge in a specific area, making your collection more meaningful and potentially more profitable in the long run. It also means you'll spend time waiting for the right pieces to come along, but this patience often pays off with higher returns.

Partner with a Trusted Dealer

While the internet is a valuable resource for learning about coins, there's no substitute for building a relationship with a trusted local dealer. A good dealer can provide access to rare coins, offer expert advice, and help authenticate and appraise your collection. Online platforms may offer convenience, but they often lack the personal touch and reliability that come with working with a dealer who knows your interests and needs.

Adopt an Investor's Mindset

To be successful in coin collecting, it's important to think like an investor. This means staying informed about market trends, understanding the value of the coins you're interested in, and knowing when to buy and when to hold. Avoid the temptation to chase quick profits; instead, focus on building a collection that will appreciate over time. Holding onto quality coins until the market conditions are favorable can lead to significantly higher returns.

Prioritize Quality Over Quantity

In the world of coin collecting, quality always trumps quantity. It's better to have a smaller collection of high-quality, visually appealing coins than a large collection of mediocre ones. Coins with minimal eye appeal are difficult to sell, and they often detract from the overall value of your collection. When acquiring new coins, be meticulous in your selection process, and always prioritize coins that are in excellent condition, even if they come with a higher price tag.

Follow Your Instincts and Interests

Collecting coins should be a pursuit of passion. Always let your interests and instincts guide your purchases. If a coin doesn't appeal to you or doesn't fit into your collection's theme, it's better to pass on it, even if it seems like a good deal. Trust your instincts and only add coins to your collection that truly resonate with you. This approach not only ensures that you enjoy your collection but also helps maintain its integrity and coherence.

Regularly Evaluate Your Collection

Regular evaluation is crucial for maintaining and enhancing the value of your collection. Understanding how to accurately assess the value of your coins is essential. This involves considering factors such as the type, condition, age, availability, and demand for each coin. By staying informed and regularly reassessing your collection, you can ensure that you're making the most of your investment and avoiding common pitfalls like underpricing or overpricing.

Exercise Patience

Patience is a virtue in coin collecting. The market for rare and valuable coins doesn't move quickly, and it often takes time to find the right pieces to add to your collection. Rushing into purchases or sales can lead to mistakes and missed opportunities. By being patient, you're more likely to make informed decisions that result in a collection that exceeds your expectations.

Commit to Continuous Learning

The world of coin collecting is vast and ever-changing, so there's always something new to learn. Whether you're a beginner or an experienced collector, staying curious and committed to learning will only enhance your experience and success. Understanding the basics of grading, knowing how to spot a cleaned or altered coin, and being aware of market trends are all essential skills that will serve you well as you build and maintain your collection.

Create and Follow a Plan

Having a clear plan for your coin collection is vital. This plan should outline your goals, the types of coins you're interested in, and your strategy for buying and selling. Sticking to your plan helps you stay focused, avoid impulsive purchases, and make informed decisions based on market conditions. A well-executed plan allows you to adapt to market fluctuations and ensures that each purchase is purpose-driven, enhancing the overall quality and value of your collection.

Keep a Detailed Catalog

Maintaining a detailed catalog of your collection is an essential part of being an organized and successful coin collector. This catalog should include all relevant information about each coin, such as the date of purchase, source, price, grading details, minting year, country, mint mark, denomination, variety, and condition. A well-kept catalog not only helps you manage your collection more effectively but also adds value when it comes time for appraisal or sale.

In conclusion, following these proven strategies can significantly enhance your experience and success as a coin collector. While these guidelines won't make the process faster, they will make it more enjoyable and rewarding. By focusing on quality, being patient, and continually learning, you can build a collection that not only brings you joy but also serves as a valuable investment for the future. Whether you're just starting or looking to refine your existing collection, these strategies will help you navigate the world of coin collecting with confidence and expertise.

How to Monetize Your Collection: A Step-by-Step Guide

Monetizing your coin collection can be a rewarding endeavor, but it requires careful planning and strategy to maximize your returns. Here's a step-by-step guide tailored to help you turn your collection into a profitable venture:

1. Evaluate Your Collection

❖ **Organize and Identify**: Start by categorizing your coins based on their type, year, mintmark, and condition. This organization will make it easier to assess the value and prepare your collection for sale. Understanding the rarity, condition, and historical significance of each coin is crucial.

❖ **Professional Appraisal**: Consider getting your collection appraised by a professional. An appraisal provides an accurate valuation, helping you understand what your coins are worth in the current market. Make sure to get a second opinion if needed, especially if you have rare or highly valuable coins.

2. Choose the Right Selling Platform

❖ **Coin Auctions**: Selling through established coin auction houses is a popular option, especially for rare or high-value coins. Auction houses like Spink or Goldberg Coins and Collectibles offer platforms where your coins can reach a broad audience of serious collectors and investors. Online auctions can also be a good choice, offering flexibility and convenience.

❖ **Online Marketplaces**: For more common coins, consider selling on platforms like eBay or specialized online coin marketplaces. These platforms allow you to set your own prices and reach a global audience, although you'll need to manage the listings and transactions yourself.

3. Timing Your Sale

❖ **Market Trends**: Coin values fluctuate based on market trends, collector demand, and economic conditions. Stay informed about these trends to sell at the optimal time. For instance, certain coins might fetch higher prices during periods of economic uncertainty when collectors and investors seek tangible assets like precious metals.

❖ **Seasonal Considerations**: Some coins sell better at certain times of the year, particularly around major coin shows or numismatic events. Timing your sale to coincide with these events can attract more attention and potentially higher bids.

4. Preserve and Present Your Collection

❖ **Proper Handling**: Ensure your coins are stored and handled correctly to maintain their condition. Use appropriate holders, avoid touching the surfaces with bare hands, and keep them in a controlled environment to prevent damage.

❖ **Detailed Cataloging**: Create a detailed catalog of your collection, including high-quality photographs, descriptions, and any relevant historical information. This not only helps in marketing your collection but also adds credibility and value in the eyes of potential buyers.

5. Negotiate and Close the Sale

❖ **Set Realistic Prices**: Based on your appraisal and market research, set realistic prices for your coins. Be prepared to negotiate, especially in private sales or auctions. Knowing the minimum price you're willing to accept will help you stay firm during negotiations.

❖ **Finalize the Sale**: Once you've agreed on a price, ensure that the transaction is secure. If selling online, use a trusted platform that offers buyer and seller protection. For in-person sales, consider using escrow services to safeguard both parties.

By following these steps, you can effectively monetize your coin collection while ensuring that you receive the best possible return on your investment. Whether you're selling a single coin or an entire collection, careful preparation and informed decision-making are key to success in the numismatic market.

Understanding Market Cycles and Timing Your Investments

Understanding market cycles and timing your investments is crucial for maximizing returns, especially in the dynamic world of coin collecting. Market cycles typically move through four phases: accumulation, mark-up, distribution, and mark-down. Recognizing where the market is within this cycle can help you make strategic decisions about when to buy, hold, or sell your coins.

1. Accumulation Phase: This is when the market has bottomed out, and savvy investors begin to buy in, recognizing that prices are likely as low as they will go. For coin collectors, this phase presents an opportunity to purchase coins at lower prices before demand picks up.

2. Mark-Up Phase: As the market gains momentum, more investors jump in, driving prices higher. During this phase, early investments can see significant appreciation. However, it's important to monitor the market carefully as it nears its peak.

3. Distribution Phase: In this phase, market sentiment becomes mixed, and prices may begin to plateau. This is when experienced investors start to sell off their holdings to lock in gains. For coin collectors, this might be the time to consider selling high-demand coins before prices start to decline.

4. Mark-Down Phase: The market begins to decline as the latecomers realize they are holding overvalued assets. Prices drop, and the cycle prepares to start again. This phase can be challenging for those who bought at the peak, but it also offers opportunities to acquire coins that may have been out of reach during the previous phases.

Understanding these cycles is key to timing your investments effectively. For instance, during a market downturn, competition for coins typically decreases, allowing for better negotiation and acquisition of rare pieces at favorable prices. Conversely, in a booming market, it might be wise to focus on selling coins that have appreciated significantly, taking advantage of high demand.

Additionally, external factors such as **inflation, interest rates**, and **global economic conditions** play significant roles in shaping these cycles. Inflation often drives collectors towards tangible assets like coins, seen as a hedge against currency devaluation. Monitoring these broader economic trends can provide further insights into where the market cycle is headed and how best to position your investments.

By staying informed and strategically timing your investments based on market cycles, you can enhance both the profitability and enjoyment of your coin collection.

PART III: THE ART OF BUYING AND SELLING COINS

CHAPTER 5

Purchasing and Trading Coins

Effective Strategies for Buying and Selling Coins

Whether you're buying or selling coins, understanding the nuances of the coin market is essential to maximizing your success. The relationship between collectors and dealers often hinges on trust and knowledge, making it crucial to equip yourself with a solid understanding of how the market operates behind the scenes.

Understanding the Coin Market

The coin market is divided primarily between wholesalers and retailers. Wholesalers are focused on acquiring coins in bulk, often attending coin shows, auctions, and advertising widely to bring new material into the market. Their main goal is to buy coins at lower prices to sell them to retail dealers, who then sell to individual collectors. Because wholesalers operate on bulk transactions, they typically offer lower prices for coins to ensure profitability when they sell to retailers.

Retail coin dealers, on the other hand, sell directly to individual collectors. These dealers might also purchase coins from wholesalers but are generally more willing to pay higher prices to acquire quality coins that they can sell to their customers. However, not all retail dealers are equal—some may be more reputable than others, and it's important to work with dealers who adhere to industry standards and ethics, such as those who are members of organizations like the American Numismatic Association.

Strategies for Buying Coins

❖ **Know the Wholesale Prices**: One of the best ways to ensure you're getting a fair deal when buying coins is to understand the wholesale prices. Publications like the Coin Dealer Newsletter, often referred to as the "Grey Sheet," provide a baseline for what dealers pay for coins. While you might not be able to buy coins at these prices, knowing them gives you leverage in negotiations and helps you avoid overpaying.

❖ **Focus on Quality**: When buying coins, prioritize quality over quantity. High-quality coins, particularly those in good grades or with strong eye appeal, tend to appreciate more over time and are easier to sell. Avoid the temptation to buy cheaper, lower-quality coins, as these often have less potential for value growth.

❖ **Develop Relationships with Trusted Dealers**: Building a relationship with a reputable dealer can be invaluable. A good dealer will offer advice, help you find specific coins, and provide fair prices for both buying and selling. They are also more likely to stand by their products and offer recourse if something goes wrong.

Strategies for Selling Coins

❖ **Timing is Key**: Just as with any investment, timing plays a crucial role in maximizing profits when selling coins. Monitor market trends, economic conditions, and collector demand to determine the best time to sell. For example, during periods of economic uncertainty, tangible assets like rare coins often see increased demand.

❖ **Sort and Catalog Your Coins**: Before selling, organize your coins by type, date, and condition. This not only makes it easier for a dealer to assess your collection but also helps you identify any particularly valuable pieces. Coins that are well-preserved in their original holders or albums generally fetch higher prices.

❖ **Understand Dealer Profit Margins**: Dealers need to make a profit to stay in business, so it's important to understand their perspective. For common coins, dealers might need to offer lower prices due to the difficulty of reselling them. Conversely, rare and high-value coins can command higher offers. Be realistic about what you can expect based on the coin's condition and market demand.

❖ **Avoid Common Pitfalls**: When selling, beware of offers that seem too low. Some dealers might make a quick assessment of a collection and offer a bulk price without thoroughly evaluating each coin. To avoid being underpaid, consider getting multiple offers or working with a dealer who takes the time to properly assess the value of your collection.

By arming yourself with knowledge and carefully considering each step in the buying and selling process, you can make more informed decisions that enhance the value and enjoyment of your coin collection. Whether you're a novice collector or a seasoned investor, these strategies will help you navigate the complexities of the coin market with confidence.

Insider Tips for Finding Rare Coins

Finding rare coins can be a thrilling pursuit, but it requires more than just luck—you need knowledge, strategy, and a keen eye for detail. While it's true that occasionally finding a valuable coin in everyday places like your couch is possible, your chances improve significantly when you know where to look and what to look for.

Understanding What Makes a Coin Rare

Before diving into where to find rare coins, it's essential to understand the characteristics that make a coin valuable. A coin typically gains rarity and value if it:

- ❖ Is no longer in production and thus decreasing in circulation.
- ❖ Is difficult to find due to limited editions or specific minting errors.
- ❖ Bears historical significance.
- ❖ Has unique markings, errors, or design features.
- ❖ Is highly sought after by collectors due to any of these factors.

Where to Search for Rare Coins

- ❖ **Explore Uncommon Places**: The best places to find rare coins are often those that have been overlooked for years. Consider searching old homes—inside walls, attics, or basements can be treasure troves. Outdoor areas like backyards, parks, and even creeks or fountains can also yield surprises, especially if they are near historical sites.

- ❖ **Bank Rolls**: A classic but effective method is to exchange paper money for rolls of coins from banks. Many collectors have found rare coins simply by sifting through these rolls. It's a low-cost way to hunt for coins that may have slipped back into circulation.

- ❖ **Metal Detecting**: Investing in a metal detector can significantly boost your chances of finding hidden treasures in large outdoor areas. Beaches, old parks, and historical landmarks are excellent places to start.

- ❖ **Ask Friends and Family**: Sometimes, the rarest coins are closer than you think. Ask family members or friends if they have old coins lying around that they might be willing to let you examine. If you find something valuable, consider offering to share the proceeds if you sell it.

- ❖ **Garage and Estate Sales**: These sales are often a goldmine for finding rare coins. Sellers might not know the true value of what they have, allowing you to acquire valuable coins at a fraction of their worth. Always be on the lookout for coin collections that have been passed down through generations.

- ❖ **Use Change Machines**: Coin-counting machines at banks and grocery stores can also be sources of rare coins. People often unknowingly deposit valuable coins, and these machines can give you access to them.

- ❖ **Online Auctions and Stores**: While less about "finding" in the traditional sense, online platforms can offer rare coins if you know what you're looking for. They allow you to browse a wide selection of coins and sometimes find undervalued gems.

Verifying Your Finds

Once you've found a coin that you suspect might be rare, the next step is verification. Researching the coin's value is critical. Several reputable websites provide valuable resources for this:

- ❖ **PCGS CoinFacts** and **NGC Coin Explorer** offer comprehensive databases that include coin values, historical context, and grading information.

❖ **Heritage Auctions and NumisMedia Fair Market Value Price Guide** are also valuable tools for determining current market values and past auction prices.

By using these resources, you can confirm the authenticity and value of your coins, ensuring that you fully understand what you've discovered.

Final Thoughts

Finding rare coins is as much about strategy and knowledge as it is about chance. By searching in overlooked places, using the right tools, and conducting thorough research, you can increase your chances of uncovering valuable coins. Always remember to verify your finds through reputable sources to ensure that you maximize the potential of your collection. Whether you're a seasoned collector or a beginner, these insider tips can help you navigate the exciting world of rare coin hunting.

CHAPTER 6

Cataloging and Managing Your Collection

Creating a System for Cataloging Your Coins

Creating a system for cataloging your coin collection is an essential practice that helps you organize and track your investments in numismatics, ensuring that your collection is well-managed and its value accurately recorded. Whether you're a seasoned collector or someone who has just inherited a collection, implementing a structured cataloging system will provide long-term benefits, not only for you but also for future generations.

The Importance of Cataloging

Cataloging your coin collection is more than just keeping track of what you own—it's about preserving the history and value of each coin. A well-documented collection allows you to monitor the performance of your investments, ensuring that you have a clear understanding of the value of your coins. Moreover, a detailed catalog will be invaluable to your heirs, helping them manage or liquidate the collection if necessary, and providing the documentation needed for tax purposes. Without proper records, your heirs might struggle to realize the full value of the collection or face challenges from tax authorities.

Methods for Cataloging Your Coins

There are several methods to catalog your coins, each offering different levels of detail and convenience. Choose the one that best suits your needs and the size of your collection.

- ❖ **Documentation in Notebooks**: For smaller collections, a simple notebook can be an effective tool for cataloging. By creating columns for each coin's country, year, mint mark, denomination, grade, purchase date, and price, you can maintain a detailed record. This method is straightforward and accessible but may become cumbersome for larger collections.

- ❖ **Acquisition Checklists**: These are pre-made lists that allow you to check off coins as you acquire them, organized by type, denomination, year, and mint mark. While checklists provide structure, they often lack space for additional information like purchase price or current value. You may need to supplement them with your notes to ensure comprehensive records.

- ❖ **Spreadsheets**: Using spreadsheet software like Microsoft Excel provides a more dynamic way to manage your collection. Spreadsheets allow you to add and modify data easily, calculate totals, and even sort or filter your collection by various attributes. You can create tabs for different types of coins or albums, making it easier to organize and keep track of everything. Spreadsheets are particularly useful for larger collections and offer the flexibility to track detailed information over time.

- ❖ **Specialized Software**: The most effective option for cataloging your coin collection is to invest in software specifically designed for coin collectors. There are numerous options available, ranging from free to more expensive versions. When selecting the right software, prioritize those that are user-friendly, with clear and intuitive interfaces. It should allow you to organize your collection in a way that suits your needs, provide access to current market prices, and automatically update the value of your collection. Additionally, it's crucial to choose software that offers a fully functional trial version or a money-back guarantee, ensuring that you can test it out before committing to a purchase. Leading software options include **Collector's Assistant, Exact Change, and Coin Elite**. These tools can save you time and provide a more comprehensive overview of your collection's value.

To check out these softwares, scan the code below:

Collector's Assistant

Exact Change

Coin Elite

Final Thoughts

A systematic approach to cataloging your coin collection not only helps you stay organized but also ensures that you are prepared for future decisions regarding buying, selling, or bequeathing your coins. Regardless of the method you choose, the key is consistency and accuracy in recording information. By maintaining a detailed catalog, you safeguard the legacy of your collection and ensure its value is preserved for years to come.

Protecting, Preserving and Storing Your Coin Collection

Maintaining the value and appearance of your coin collection requires diligent attention to preservation techniques. Coins, particularly rare or valuable ones, can be easily compromised by improper handling, storage, and cleaning. Understanding the best practices for preserving your coins is crucial to keeping them in pristine condition and protecting your investment.

Proper Handling of Coins

The way you handle your coins can greatly affect their condition. Oils, dirt, and contaminants from your skin can lead to discoloration and corrosion over time. Always handle coins with care to avoid unnecessary damage.

Tips:

- ❖ **Wear Gloves**: Use clean, lint-free cotton or nitrile gloves to prevent transferring oils and dirt from your hands to the coins.
- ❖ **Hold by the Edges**: Always hold coins by their edges to minimize contact with their surfaces.
- ❖ **Soft Surface Handling**: Handle coins over a soft, clean surface to avoid damage in case of accidental drops.

Safe Storage Solutions

Proper storage is critical to protect coins from environmental damage such as humidity, temperature fluctuations, and pollutants. Selecting the right storage solutions will help maintain the condition and value of your collection.

Tips:

- ❖ **Coin Holders**: Use acid-free coin holders like flips, capsules, or cardboard holders to protect individual coins.
- ❖ **Albums and Binders**: Store coins in albums or binders with acid-free pages to organize and protect your collection.
- ❖ **Coin Boxes**: For larger collections, consider using storage boxes with compartments to keep coins separated and secure.

Environmental Control

Maintaining a stable and controlled environment is key to the long-term preservation of your coins.

Tips:

- ❖ **Humidity Control**: Keep humidity levels between 30% and 50% to prevent corrosion and tarnish. Use silica gel packs or a dehumidifier if necessary.
- ❖ **Temperature Stability**: Store coins in a cool, stable environment away from direct sunlight to avoid temperature fluctuations and UV damage.
- ❖ **Air Quality**: Maintain optimal air quality in the storage area by minimizing exposure to pollutants, dust, and harmful chemicals.

Cleaning Coins Correctly

Cleaning coins can be risky and is generally discouraged unless absolutely necessary, as improper cleaning can reduce a coin's value and cause irreversible damage.

Tips:

- ❖ **Assess Necessity**: Determine if cleaning is essential. Light tarnish or natural patina should generally be left intact.

- ❖ **Professional Cleaning**: For valuable or rare coins, consider professional cleaning services from a numismatist or conservation expert.
- ❖ **Safe Cleaning Methods**: If you decide to clean a coin, rinse it gently in distilled water and dry it with a soft, lint-free cloth. Avoid using abrasive materials or chemicals.

Preventing Physical Damage

Preventing physical damage such as scratches, dents, and wear is essential for maintaining your coin collection.

Tips:

- ❖ **Soft Surfaces**: When handling coins, ensure they are placed over a soft surface, such as a clean cloth or foam pad, to protect them from damage.
- ❖ **Individual Storage**: Store coins separately in holders or compartments to prevent them from coming into contact with each other and causing friction or scratches.
- ❖ **Avoid Loose Coins**: Never carry loose coins in your pocket or bag, as they can rub against each other and cause damage.

Insurance and Documentation

Insuring your coin collection protects against loss, theft, and damage, while proper documentation is essential for insurance and maintaining accurate records.

Tips:

- ❖ **Insurance Coverage**: Obtain insurance specifically for your coin collection.
- ❖ **Detailed Inventory**: Keep a detailed inventory, including descriptions, grades, purchase prices, and photographs.
- ❖ **Secure Storage**: Store valuable coins in a safe or safety deposit box to protect them from theft and damage.

Regular Maintenance and Inspections

Establishing a routine for regular maintenance and inspections helps preserve the condition and value of your coins.

Tips:

- ❖ **Scheduled Inspections**: Inspect your coins regularly for signs of damage, discoloration, or corrosion.
- ❖ **Clean Environment**: Keep the storage area clean, dust-free, and within optimal humidity and temperature ranges.
- ❖ **Update Records**: Regularly update your inventory and records to reflect any changes in your coin collection, including condition, new acquisitions, or sales.

Displaying Your Collection

While it's important to keep your coins protected, displaying your collection can enhance your enjoyment. Use appropriate display methods that protect your coins from damage.

Tips:

- ❖ **Protective Cases**: Use display cases with UV-protective glass to shield coins from light and prevent fading.
- ❖ **Avoid Direct Sunlight**: Place display cabinets away from direct sunlight to prevent temperature fluctuations and UV damage.

By following these best practices for handling, storing, cleaning, and displaying your coins, you can ensure they remain in perfect condition for years to come. Whether you're just starting your collection or have been collecting for years, these strategies will help you protect and preserve your coins, safeguarding your investment and preserving history for future generations.

PART IV: AVOIDING SCAMS AND ENSURING AUTHENTICITY

CHAPTER 7

Spotting Counterfeit Coins

Tools and Techniques for Detecting Fake Coins

Detecting counterfeit coins is a critical skill for any serious coin collector or investor. With the growing sophistication of counterfeiters, having the right tools and techniques at your disposal is essential to protect your collection and investments. Here are some of the most effective methods and tools for identifying fake coins:

Essential Tools for Detecting Counterfeit Coins

❖ **Lighting**: Proper lighting is crucial for inspecting coins. A high-quality desk lamp with a bright white LED bulb that offers a full-color spectrum is recommended. This helps to reveal subtle differences in color and texture that might indicate a counterfeit coin.

❖ **Magnification**: Magnification tools like loupes and microscopes are indispensable. A 12X loupe is useful for quick inspections, while a stereo microscope with a zoom factor of 10X to 45X is ideal for detailed analysis. The microscope should also have built-in lighting to ensure even illumination of the coin's surface.

❖ **Scales:** A precision digital scale with an accuracy of at least 0.01 grams is necessary to measure the coin's weight. Authentic coins have specific weight standards, and deviations can be a telltale sign of a counterfeit.

❖ **Calipers**: A digital caliper accurate to 0.01 mm is used to measure the diameter and thickness of coins. Counterfeit coins often fail to match the exact dimensions of authentic pieces.

❖ **Magnet**: A strong rare-earth magnet, such as a Neodymium N52 disc, is useful for detecting counterfeit coins made with magnetic metals like iron or steel, which should not be present in genuine coins.

❖ **Metal Composition Analyzers**: Advanced tools like the Precious Metal Verifier or X-ray fluorescence (XRF) technology are used to analyze the metallic composition of a coin. These non-destructive tools are highly accurate but can be expensive. They are especially useful for verifying the authenticity of bullion coins.

Techniques for Identifying Counterfeit Coins

Visual Inspection: Begin with a thorough visual inspection under ideal lighting. Look for inconsistencies in the coin's color, texture, and design details. Compare the coin to high-resolution images of genuine coins if you're unfamiliar with the series.

❖ **Weight and Dimensions**: Use your digital scale and calipers to check the coin's weight and dimensions against known standards. Even slight deviations can indicate a counterfeit.

❖ Magnet Test: If the coin is not supposed to contain any magnetic metals, it should not be attracted to a magnet. This simple test can quickly eliminate some counterfeits.

❖ **Sound Test (Ring Test)**: Genuine coins made of certain metals, like silver, produce a distinct ringing sound when lightly tapped. Counterfeit coins, especially those made from different materials, often produce a duller sound.

❖ **Surface and Detail Analysis**: Using a microscope, examine the coin's surface for signs of casting, such as pitting or rough edges. Pay special attention to the details of the design, including the sharpness of letters and numbers, as counterfeit coins often have softer, less defined features.

❖ **Authentication Services**: For high-value or questionable coins, consider sending them to a professional grading service like NGC or PCGS. These services use advanced tools and expertise to authenticate coins and can provide a detailed analysis and certification.

By employing these tools and techniques, you can significantly reduce the risk of falling victim to counterfeit coins. Regularly educating yourself and staying updated with the latest developments in counterfeit detection will further enhance your ability to protect your collection.

The Most Common Coin Scams and How to Avoid Them

When it comes to coin collecting, understanding and avoiding common scams is crucial to protecting your investments. Here's an extensive guide on some of the most common coin scams and how you can avoid them:

1. Counterfeit Coins

One of the most prevalent scams involves counterfeit coins, where scammers produce fake coins that closely resemble genuine ones. These counterfeit coins can range from everyday coins to high-value numismatic items. The rise of online auctions and marketplaces has made it easier for counterfeiters to sell these coins, often at prices too good to be true.

How to Avoid: Always buy from reputable dealers and verify the authenticity of coins through third-party grading services like PCGS or NGC. If a deal seems too good to be true, it probably is. Be especially cautious with purchases made through online platforms.

2. Overpriced TV Shopping and Premium Mints

TV shopping channels and some premium mints often sell coins at exorbitant prices, claiming they are rare or of significant investment value. In reality, these coins are often common, mass-produced items that hold little to no premium in the numismatic market.

How to Avoid: Research before making any purchases. Compare prices with reputable coin dealers and avoid impulse buys from TV channels or glossy advertisements.

3. Spurious Sets

Scammers often assemble low-grade coins into sets and sell them at inflated prices, claiming they are rare or have historical significance. These sets are usually marketed with appealing themes, such as coins from a particular war or era, but they generally lack real value.

How to Avoid: Educate yourself on the true value of the coins included in such sets. Verify their authenticity and market value through reliable sources before making a purchase.

4. Modified Coins

Some scammers alter genuine coins by adding holographic stickers, coloring, or other modifications to make them appear rare or unique. While these modifications might make the coins visually appealing, they actually decrease their value in the numismatic market.

How to Avoid: Avoid purchasing coins that have been visibly altered. Stick to unmodified coins, especially if you're investing for future value.

5. Scams on Online Marketplaces

The anonymity and global reach of online marketplaces make them a hotbed for scams. Sellers might offer rare coins at seemingly incredible prices, but once you purchase, you either receive a counterfeit coin or nothing at all.

How to Avoid: Only purchase from sellers with verified credentials and positive reviews. Use payment methods that offer protection, and consider having the coins authenticated before finalizing a purchase.

6. Fake Grading Services

Some scammers set up fake grading services to assign inflated grades to coins, making them appear more valuable than they actually are. These fake grades can mislead buyers into overpaying for coins.

How to Avoid: Stick to coins graded by reputable services like PCGS or NGC. Always verify the grading service's credentials and look up the coin's certification number on the service's official website.

By being aware of these common scams and taking steps to protect yourself, you can enjoy coin collecting while safeguarding your investments. Always remember to do thorough research and when in doubt, consult with reputable professionals in the field. This vigilance will help ensure that your collecting experience is both enjoyable and profitable.

Using Technology to Verify Coin Authenticity

Modern technology has significantly advanced the field of coin authentication, allowing experts to use sophisticated methods to verify the authenticity of coins with high precision. One of the most powerful tools available today is **X-ray fluorescence spectroscopy** (XRF), a non-destructive technique that provides detailed information about a coin's metallic composition. This method has become a cornerstone in numismatics, especially for organizations like PCGS (Professional Coin Grading Service).

X-Ray Fluorescence Spectroscopy (XRF)

XRF technology works by directing a focused beam of X-rays at a coin, which causes the atoms in the coin to emit secondary X-rays. These emitted rays are unique to each element, allowing the technology to detect and quantify the metals present on the coin's surface.

This non-invasive technique is far superior to older methods like acid-based assays, which could damage the coin. XRF can detect even minor variations in metal composition, making it an invaluable tool for distinguishing between genuine coins and well-crafted counterfeits.

Applications in Coin Authentication

The primary use of XRF in coin authentication is to compare the metal composition of a suspect coin with that of known authentic specimens. This is particularly useful for coins from periods or regions where counterfeiting was prevalent. For example, early American, colonial, and pioneer coins are often targets for counterfeiters. XRF allows experts to detect even subtle differences in alloy compositions that are not visible to the naked eye but are crucial for verifying authenticity.

Advancements in Numismatic Research

Beyond authentication, XRF technology has expanded our understanding of historical coinage. For instance, the analysis of "New Haven" restrikes of Fugio Cents from the 1860s revealed two distinct metal compositions: one nearly pure copper and the other alloyed with zinc. This discovery has led to a reassessment of these coins' origins and rarity.

Moreover, XRF has been instrumental in examining experimental coins from the U.S. Mint, such as pattern coins from the mid-19th century. These coins were struck in various metal compositions, and over time, the surface appearance could change due to patination, making visual identification challenging. XRF provides a reliable means of distinguishing between different compositions, thus aiding in the accurate cataloging and grading of these coins.

The Future of Coin Authentication

As technology advances, tools like XRF are becoming more accessible to collectors and smaller institutions. The continued integration of these technologies into the coin authentication process ensures that numismatics will remain a robust and scientifically rigorous field. By embracing these advancements, collectors can have greater confidence in the authenticity of their collections, and researchers can continue to uncover new insights into historical coinage.

Incorporating modern technology like XRF into your collecting and authentication practices will not only protect your investments but also deepen your understanding of the coins' historical and material significance.

PART V: VALUABLE ERROR COINS BY DENOMINATION

CHAPTER 8

Understanding Error Coins

Error coins are distinctive coins that feature mistakes resulting from the minting process, making them highly coveted by collectors. These errors can occur during various stages of production, such as during striking, where issues like missing mint marks or off-center strikes can arise. Planchet errors are caused by problems with the metal disc before it is minted, while die errors happen during the actual striking of the coin. Each type of error has its own unique characteristics, and understanding these differences is key to recognizing their rarity and determining their value. Interested in delving deeper into the intriguing world of error coins and learning how to spot them?

Origins of Error Coins

Error coins have captivated numismatists for generations due to their unusual origins and distinct characteristics. These coins emerge from deviations in the minting process, resulting in a variety of anomalies that collectors eagerly seek out.

Imagine holding a coin with a doubled image, where the design appears slightly shifted or duplicated—a striking error that occurs during the minting process. Or consider a planchet error, where the metal disc intended for the coin is improperly cut, leading to irregular shapes or missing details on the final coin. These imperfections add an element of intrigue and excitement to coin collecting.

Whether it's a missing mint mark, an off-center strike, or a clipped planchet, each error coin carries a unique story. By understanding the origins of these rare coins, you can appreciate the artistry and craftsmanship involved, even when unexpected deviations make them stand out.

Types of Error Coins

As you delve into the intriguing realm of error coins, you'll discover a variety of types that highlight specific anomalies in their minting process. These errors can range from subtle imperfections to significant mistakes that greatly influence the coin's rarity and value.

Each error coin possesses distinct characteristics that set it apart from regular coins. By recognizing these differences, you can gain a deeper appreciation for the rarity and significance that error coins bring to the world of numismatics.

Here are some common types of error coins you may encounter:

Type of Error	Description	Example
Planchet Errors	Problems with the coin blank before the striking process.	Blank planchet, clipped planchet, off-center strike
Die Errors	Issues with the dies used during the striking process.	Die crack, die clash, doubled die
Minting Errors	Errors that arise during the minting process.	Broadstrike, off-metal strike, repunched mint mark

Causes of Error Coins

Understanding how error coins are created provides valuable insights into the minting process and the various factors that contribute to these unique and collectible anomalies. Several factors can result in the production of error coins:

* ❖ **Minting Defects**: Issues that arise during the striking process, such as misaligned dies or incorrect pressure, can cause errors like off-center strikes or double strikes.
* ❖ **Die Errors**: Problems in the production or maintenance of dies can lead to errors such as doubled dies, where parts of the design appear duplicated.
* ❖ **Planchet Issues**: Complications with planchets, including incorrect metal composition, thickness variations, or the presence of contaminants, can result in errors like blank or clipped planchets.

These factors underscore the complexity of the minting process and the potential for errors that create these rare and sought-after coins. By understanding these causes, collectors and numismatists can more fully appreciate the rarity and distinctiveness of error coins in the numismatic world.

Detecting Error Coins

To identify error coins, closely examine the coin's features for any deviations from standard minting characteristics. Begin by checking the date, mintmark, and design elements for accuracy. Pay particular attention to the strike quality, which indicates how well the design details were imprinted onto the coin. Errors such as weak strikes or double strikes can lead to a lack of sharpness in the design. Additionally, inspect the coin's planchet—the metal disc used before striking—for any irregularities like cracks, laminations, or clips, as these can cause visible abnormalities on the final coin.

Next, look for signs of doubling, missing elements, or misplaced designs. Double dies can cause parts of the design to appear duplicated, while missing elements might indicate a filled die error, where portions of the design are obscured. Misplaced designs occur when the design elements are not correctly aligned on the coin. By carefully examining these aspects, you can effectively identify error coins within your collection.

Collecting Error Coins

Consider diversifying your collection by incorporating error coins, as they can bring a unique and valuable dimension to your numismatic holdings. Error coins captivate collectors due to their unusual features, which arise from mistakes during the minting process. These coins can range from minor flaws like off-center strikes to significant errors such as double strikes or missing mintmarks, making them a fascinating and worthwhile addition to any collection.

Investing in Error Coins

Expand your investment portfolio by exploring the unique and valuable potential of error coins in the numismatic market. Error coins can offer significant financial returns while adding an intriguing element to your collection. Here's why investing in error coins could be a profitable decision:

- ❖ **Rarity and Uniqueness**: Error coins stand out due to production mistakes, making them rare and highly prized among collectors.
- ❖ **Potential for High Returns**: The scarcity of these coins often drives up their value over time, offering the possibility of substantial gains on your investment.
- ❖ **Strong Collector Demand**: Error coins attract a dedicated group of collectors passionate about these one-of-a-kind pieces, ensuring ongoing market demand.

Incorporating error coins into your investment strategy can diversify your portfolio and potentially yield significant rewards from this captivating segment of the numismatic world.

Future of Error Coins

Exploring the future potential of error coins can offer valuable insights into emerging trends and opportunities within the numismatic market. With advancements in technology and increasingly sophisticated minting processes, the chances of new and unique error coins being produced are likely to rise. This presents exciting opportunities for collectors and investors to discover rare pieces that could hold substantial value in the future.

The outlook for error coins appears promising, as technological progress in minting may lead to the creation of even more intriguing errors. This development opens up new avenues for investment for those interested in acquiring distinctive additions to their collections. However, as the market continues to expand, challenges such as ensuring authentication and managing market fluctuations will be critical to maintaining the success and integrity of error coin collecting.

CHAPTER 9

Valuable Error Pennies

Collecting penny errors is an exciting hobby, as these coins can vary widely in value. If you know what to look for, you might stumble upon a valuable Lincoln penny with a rare error still circulating in everyday use.

Determining the value of an error penny isn't straightforward, as it depends on several factors. The overall worth of an error coin is influenced by its condition, rarity, and the extent of the error. These variables make each error penny unique, and its value can range from modest to significant depending on these characteristics.

Top Error Pennies Worth Money

1. 1983 Penny Doubled Die Reverse

The doubling effect on the reverse side of the 1983 penny resulted from an issue during the hubbing process, specifically due to a misalignment between the die and the working hub. This doubling is typically noticeable on the lettering of the coin.

The more pronounced and visible the doubling, the higher the coin's value tends to be. For example, a red MS 68 DDR (Double Die Reverse) penny can fetch a remarkable price, with one such coin selling for as much as $7,050.

2. 1969 S Double Die Obverse Penny

This is one of the most famous and highly sought-after errors in the Lincoln coin series.

First discovered by collectors Bill Hudson and Ceil Moorhouse in the 1970s, this doubled die error has been a target for many counterfeit attempts.

At one point, the U.S. Secret Service even confiscated 1969 S pennies suspected of having this error to crack down on counterfeit currency. While the genuine coins were eventually returned to their owners, many 1969 S pennies with the error were destroyed in the process.

Today, this error coin is extremely rare, with only about 40 to 50 known examples. The most recent discovery was made in 2007.

The doubling effect is clearly visible around the words "LIBERTY," "IN GOD WE TRUST," and the date.

A coin graded by PCGS as MS-64 Red with this error was valued at an astounding $126,500.

3. 1998 Wide AM Penny

The 1998 Lincoln penny has an intriguing history that has made it particularly popular among collectors. The error occurred when Mint workers mistakenly used a reverse die intended for proof coins to strike the reverse of a circulation penny.

This minting mistake is also found in 1999 and 2000 circulation strike Lincoln cents, with the 1998 version being the rarest. Due to the reuse of multiple dies, over 100,000 pennies were struck with this error.

To identify whether a Lincoln penny was struck with a proof reverse die, examine the spacing between the letters "AM" in the word "AMERICA." On business strike coins dated from 1993 to 2008, the letters "AM" are close together, while on proof coins dated from 1994 to 2008, the "AM" letters are noticeably separated.

While 1998 wide AM pennies are relatively common in circulated condition, finding them in mint state is much more difficult. Coins graded MS68 or higher are extremely rare and command high prices in the market. Collectors can expect to pay $5,000 or more for a 1998 wide AM Lincoln penny graded MS67 or above.

4. 1998 Close AM Penny

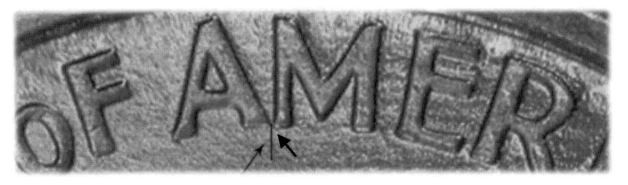

Some 1998 penny proofs feature a noticeable Close AM, which was not the intention of the U.S. Mint. These coins were meant to be struck with the Wide AM die for collectors, so those with the Close AM are considered error coins.

You can purchase a 1998 DCAM (Deep Cameo) red Memorial cent proof in grades PR 66 to PR 69 for anywhere between $100 and $275. As is often the case, auction prices can be significantly higher. For example, two PR 70-graded pieces were sold on eBay for $4,500 in 2015 and $4,000 in 2018.

5. 1998 D Doubled Die Penny

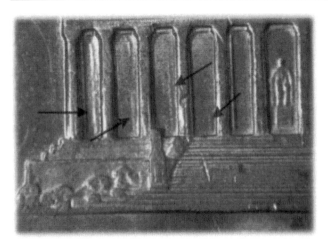 

Pennies with this error exhibit unintended doubling of numbers, letters, or images, typically on one side of the coin. This occurs due to a design flaw during the die's production, leading to the doubling effect.

You might notice doubling in areas such as Lincoln's eye, his bowtie, parts of the lettering, or the pillars of the Memorial. In most cases, the doubling is minor on coins minted in this year and can only be seen with a magnifying glass. These error coins generally sell for $20 to $50.

6. 1992 Wide and Close AM Penny

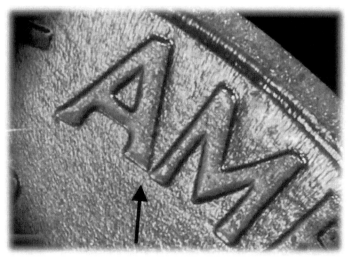

The wide and close AM error is one of the most recognized errors found in Lincoln Memorial pennies, particularly those minted in 1992. This error pertains to the spacing between the letters "A" and "M" in the word "AMERICA" on the coin's reverse. On some coins, the gap between these letters is notably wide, while on others, the letters are positioned so closely that they almost touch.

In addition to the AM spacing, Frank Gasparro's initials on the reverse can also show variations. In some close AM pennies, his initials are spaced apart, while in some wide AM pennies, the initials are placed closely together.

Both wide and close AM errors can be found on the 1992 no-mint mark and 1992-D pennies. However, close AM errors are much rarer, making them more valuable.

According to the Professional Coin Grading Service (PCGS), a 1992 no-mint mark penny with a close AM error, graded by the Numismatic Guaranty Company (NGC) as genuine, sold for $5,000 in a 2022 online auction. Additionally, a close AM 1992-D penny graded as About Uncirculated (AU) 58 fetched $3,525 at a Stack's Bowers auction in 2012.

7. 1970-S Small Date Penny

These pennies quickly garnered significant attention, becoming some of the most sought-after coins in the Lincoln cent series.

The 1970-S Small Date penny is particularly rare, with collectors often dedicating years to searching through rolls of coins and pocket change to find them. Even when found in circulated condition, these pennies are worth more than their face value, and those in mint state can command prices in the three-figure range, depending on their grade.

There are two primary ways to distinguish a Small Date Lincoln cent from a Large Date version. The first method involves examining the date itself. On Small Date coins, the top of the number 7 aligns with the other digits (1, 9, and 0). Conversely, on Large Date coins, the 7 is positioned slightly lower than the other numbers.

Another distinguishing factor is the word "LIBERTY." On Large Date pennies, this word appears strong and well-defined, whereas on Small Date varieties, it often appears weaker and less pronounced.

The most valuable 1970-S Small Date Lincoln penny was sold for an impressive $18,400. This particular coin was graded PF69 and awarded Deep Cameo status, highlighting its exceptional quality and rarity.

8. 1970-D Penny Struck 55% Off-Centre

Coins are created by stamping designs onto blank metal discs known as planchets. A die is used to strike the planchet, but sometimes the planchet can shift before the first strike, resulting in a portion of the coin's surface being unmarked. This type of error is known as a misalignment or off-center error and is typically described in terms of the percentage of the design that is missing. For example, a coin struck 55% off-center is one such case. While interesting, these errors aren't always highly valuable; a coin in MS 63 RD condition with a 55% off-center strike recently sold for $65.

9. 1972 Doubled Die Obverse

 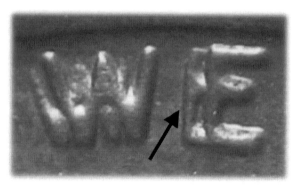

When a cent is struck by the dies two or more times, the result is a noticeable doubling of the design on the obverse. This error is particularly evident in 1972 pennies, where the most common areas of doubling appear in the words "LIBERTY," "IN GOD WE TRUST," and the date "1972." Although such errors are relatively common, they still hold considerable value. Depending on the color and condition of the penny, its price can range from $295 to as much as $14,400.

10. 1909 VDB Wheat Penny DDO

A double die error is found in both variations of the 1909 Lincoln penny, with and without the VDB initials. This error, caused by a doubling of design elements during the minting process, is particularly noticeable on the word "LIBERTY." Experts estimate that around 500 VDB pennies from 1909 were produced with this error. These error coins are typically valued at about $1,000, although auction prices can be significantly higher. The most notable sale was a 1909 VDB penny with a double die obverse (DDO) error, graded MS 67+ red, which fetched $31,200 at auction in 2023.

11. 1909 Wheat Penny RPM

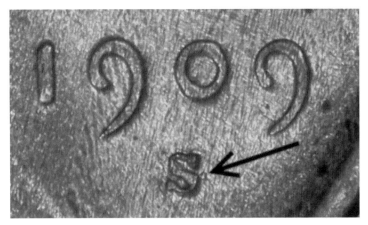

Some 1909 Wheat pennies feature a re-punched mint mark error, where you can observe an "S" over a horizontal "S" on the obverse. This error occurred when the mint mark was incorrectly struck the first time, and a second attempt was made to correct it.

These error pennies generally command about 10% more than their regular counterparts, though auction prices can be significantly higher. For example, in 2018, a brown-colored error penny sold for $875, while a red-brown version reached $1,668 in 2006. The most expensive was a red specimen graded MS 67, which fetched an impressive $32,900 at auction in 2022.

12. 1943 Bronze Cent

The 1943 transition error is one of the rarest Mint errors, occurring when a coin is mistakenly struck on an old type of planchet. In 1943, a few pennies were accidentally struck on the traditional bronze planchets instead of the new steel and zinc ones. These error coins are highly collectible and valuable in any condition.

Bronze coins are graded as brown, red and brown, or red, depending on the brightness of the copper. Generally, brown coins are the least expensive, while red coins fetch the highest prices.

The Professional Coin Grading Service (PCGS) has certified ten bronze 1943 pennies in brown, with grades ranging from XF45 to MS62. The XF45 is valued at $215,000, while the two MS62 examples are each worth around $435,000.

Additionally, there is a single red and brown coin graded MS61, valued at $425,000. The finest known example is a red coin graded MS63, which the PCGS values at an impressive $1 million.

13. 1943 D/D Steel Penny, Re-punched Mint Mark

 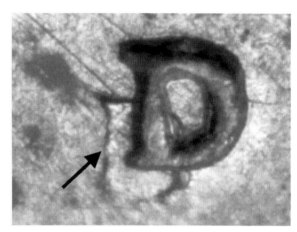

In 1943, mint marks were applied to coins manually, and occasionally, a second mint mark was inadvertently punched over the first. This error is evident in some 1943 steel pennies minted in Denver, where the faint outline of the original "D" can be seen beneath the more prominent, second strike.

These error coins are highly sought after by collectors, with values depending largely on their condition. Even in lower grades, these coins hold significant value. For instance, a coin graded "Good" 4 is valued at $55 by the PCGS, with the value increasing to $175 for a coin graded XF45.

In mint condition, the value jumps significantly. A coin graded MS60 is estimated to be worth around $425, while the auction record for this error was set in 2011 when an MS67 example sold for an impressive $21,275.

14. 1917 Wheat Penny DDO

The 1917 Double Die Obverse pennies are highly sought after by collectors due to their rarity and collectible status, which makes them quite valuable. Even circulated examples can command prices ranging from $100 to $2,640. Coins in mint state condition are even more expensive, with values estimated between $2,750 and $7,200.

Red-brown coins are particularly prized, with prices ranging from $6,500 to $10,500, depending on the grade (MS 63 to MS 65). However, the most desirable are the red-toned cents from 1917. These are estimated to be worth:

- MS 63: $8,000 to $9,600
- MS 64: $10,500 to $12,600
- MS 65: $15,000 to $18,000
- MS 66: $25,000 to $30,000
- MS 67: $85,000 to $100,000

Auction results often exceed these estimates, with the highest recorded price being an astounding $120,000 for a 1917 MS 67+ red penny with a Double Die Obverse (DDO) error, achieved in 2019. This makes it the most valuable coin in this series.

15. 1925 S Penny, Re-punched Mint Marks

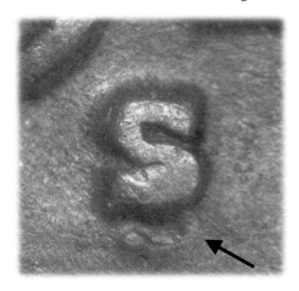

Another error found on some 1925 S pennies is a re-punched mint mark, where the lower curve of the first "S" can be faintly seen beneath the second. The value of these coins depends largely on their condition. A brown example in the lowest grade might fetch around $27, with prices increasing to $120 for an XF45 and $260 for an MS60.

The most valuable re-punched mint mark 1925 S penny certified so far is a red coin graded MS65, which the Professional Coin Grading Service (PCGS) values at an impressive $43,000.

16. 1955 Wheat Penny Double Die Obverse

The 1955 Wheat penny with a double die obverse is one of the most renowned error coins. Approximately 40,000 of these coins were produced in a single night at the Philadelphia Mint, leading to a highly sought-after numismatic rarity. But how did this error occur, and how can it be identified?

Double die errors happen during the creation of the die that imprints the design onto coins. The die receives the image through repeated strikes from a hub. If there's any slight movement between these strikes, it results in a doubled image on the die, which is then transferred to the coins it produces.

The 1955 Wheat pennies struck that night display this doubling prominently on the obverse, especially on the date and inscriptions. There's also some loss of detail on Lincoln's bust, though it is less noticeable.

Before the error was discovered, around 22,000 of these coins entered circulation. Finding one in mint condition is exceptionally rare. For instance, a brown 1955 double die penny sold for $1,500 at auction in March 2019. A red version of this coin in MS60 condition is valued by the PCGS at $3,250, and at MS65, its value skyrockets to $52,500.

The top two known specimens, graded MS65+, are valued at an incredible $288,000 each by the PCGS.

Due to the coin's fame, many fakes exist. Therefore, it's crucial to ensure that any purchase is authenticated by reputable organizations like the PCGS or NGC before investing significant money.

17. 1900 No Mint Mark Indian Head Penny, Repunched Date

There are three distinct varieties of 1900 business strike pennies that feature a repunched date.

In the first variety, the repunching is quite subtle, with the original digit barely noticeable. Look closely for a faint line curving northeast from the final "0," which is the remnant of the original digit.

The second variety exhibits repunching on the top of the "1," the middle of the "9," and the top of the second "0." This variety is difficult to detect with the naked eye and often requires a microscope or loupe for proper identification.

The third variety, certified exclusively by the NGC, is perhaps the most distinct. Here, the original "9" is visible to the left and below the final digit, and the bottom part of the first "0" can be seen beneath the final digit.

The value of these varieties depends on the coin's condition. While there is limited pricing history for the third variety, the first two varieties have established values: a coin graded VF20 is worth about $45, at AU58 it fetches around $100, and a red and brown coin graded MS65 is valued at approximately $450.

18. 1859 Re-Punched Date Penny

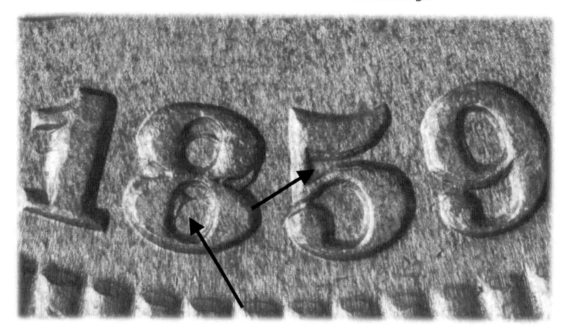

This type of error is quite common among pennies minted in 1859, primarily due to the fact that mint workers manually stamped the dates onto the coins. This manual process led to a wide range of errors, from subtle imperfections to those that are easily noticeable. The value of these coins can vary significantly based on the visibility of the error, typically ranging from $10 to $60 per coin.

However, auction records tell a different story, with some coins fetching prices between $1,980 and $6,600. The final price often depends on the location of the error and how prominently it is displayed on the coin.

19. 1877 Strike-Through Indian Head Penny

Strike-through errors are relatively common in 1877 Indian Head pennies. This type of error happens when a foreign object, such as grease, debris, or dust particles, gets between the planchet (the blank coin) and the dies during the minting process. This obstruction prevents the die from fully imprinting the design onto the planchet, leading to a strike-through error.

The value of a strike-through error can vary widely depending on the size and impact of the obstruction. Larger obstructions that cause significant portions of the design to be missing can be more valuable, especially if the coin's date remains visible. An 1877 Indian Head penny with a noticeable strike-through error can fetch between $1,000 and $2,000, depending on the extent of the error and the coin's overall condition.

20. 1908 Indian Head Penny Misplaced Date

A misplaced date on a coin occurs when there's a faint re-stamp of the numerals representing the date, positioned slightly off from the actual mintage year. For example, a 1908 penny with this error might initially appear normal, but closer inspection with a magnifying glass reveals the subtle anomaly.

This error likely happens because a Mint employee tested the date die on the edge of the coin to ensure it was working properly. Since the edge is typically covered by the coin's denticles, it was probably assumed that no one would notice the faint secondary date stamp.

The year 1908 was the last year that dates were manually punched into master dies, making misplaced or "repunched" dates more common for coins from this era. An MS65 Brown 1908 Indian Head penny featuring this intriguing error once sold for approximately $100.

21. 1888 Indian Penny 8/7 Overdate

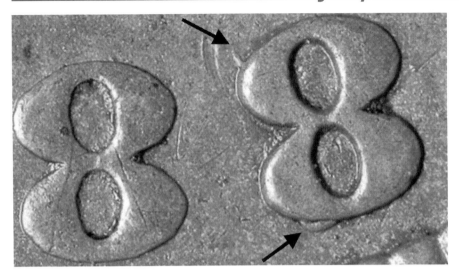

An overdate error occurs when one mint date is stamped over a previous year's date on a coin. In this case, it's an 1888 date struck over an 1887, where traces of the "7" can still be seen beneath the final "8." This kind of error is classified as a variety, meaning the mistake occurred on the die and was replicated on every coin produced from that die. The value of these coins can be quite high, with an AU 58 BN example selling for $43,200 in 2021, an MS 63 BN fetching $74,750 in 2007, and an MS 64 RB reaching $72,000 in 2019.

CHAPTER 10

Valuable Nickel Errors

Is collecting nickels worth your time? If you have an old or unusual-looking nickel, you might be wondering if it holds any value beyond its face value.

The United States Mint has been producing nickels since 1866, with the Jefferson nickel, minted since 1938, being the most common modern version. Generally, most people don't view nickels as particularly valuable, and in many cases, they're only worth their face value. However, the real treasures lie in nickel errors, which can be surprisingly valuable.

Many older nickels have become rare since they're no longer in circulation, and those with unique minting errors are even rarer and can be highly valuable.

In this overview of nickel errors, we'll explore some of the most valuable ones. By the end, you'll know what to watch for in your pocket change to see if you might have a rare and valuable nickel.

Top Error Nickels Worth Money

1. 1937 D Three-Legged Buffalo Nickel

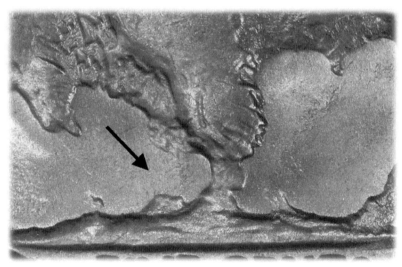

In 1937, the Denver Mint produced a limited number of nickels that became famously known as "Three-Legged Buffalos." These nickels got their name because the buffalo on the reverse side appears to be missing a front leg. This distinctive feature wasn't a deliberate design choice but rather the result of excessive polishing of the reverse die. The polishing process caused the front foreleg to almost entirely vanish, leaving behind a faint mark under the buffalo's stomach, often described as a "stream." Additionally, the back leg has a worn, slightly deteriorated look.

Because of their rarity, genuine Three-Legged Buffalo nickels are highly sought after and command significant value. Even in lower grades, such as a grade of 15, these nickels can be worth around $650. For a better-preserved example, graded XF45, the value jumps to approximately $1,000. Uncirculated examples start at about $2,950.

The most pristine examples certified by the Professional Coin Grading Service (PCGS) are five coins graded MS66+, one of which fetched nearly $100,000 in 2021. The current value of an MS66+ Three-Legged Buffalo nickel is estimated at $105,000. Meanwhile, the Numismatic Guaranty Corporation (NGC) has graded three examples at MS67, with each valued at an impressive $150,000.

It's important to be cautious, as many fake Three-Legged Buffalo nickels are on the market. Identifying the specific characteristics of genuine coins, such as the missing foreleg and the faint stream under the buffalo, is crucial for collectors.

2. 1937 D Over D Buffalo Nickel, Repunched Mint Mark

Some of the 1937 Buffalo nickels produced at the Denver Mint feature an error known as a "repunched mint mark." If you examine the mint mark closely on the reverse, you might notice the faint impression of a second "D" beneath the primary one.

While this type of error isn't exceedingly rare, it does increase the coin's value. For example, a Buffalo nickel with this error graded MS65 sold at auction for $150, which is approximately 50% more than a similar coin without the error at the same grade.

A similar repunched mint mark error can also be found on some San Francisco Buffalo nickels. One such coin, also graded MS65, fetched $185 at auction, reflecting the added value that this error brings to collectors.

3. 1935 D Re-punched Mint Mark

Buffalo nickels from Denver occasionally feature a re-punched mint mark, where the second "D" can be found either within the first mark or slightly offset to the left or right. The value of these coins ranges from $80 to $550, depending on the visibility of the error and the coin's overall condition. The highest price ever recorded for a D/D Buffalo nickel at auction was $999, achieved in June 2013.

4. 1964 Four Strikes and Three Off-Centre Nickel

During the minting process, coins typically receive multiple strikes to ensure that the design is fully impressed onto the blank planchet. However, in this particular case, an error occurred where the coin was struck four times, with three of these strikes being off-center due to an unstable die. This error is quite rare, and the limited number of known examples, which are in good condition and rank highly on the coin-grading scale, make them highly valuable. The combination of rarity and the unique nature of this error can drive the coin's value up to $1,200.

5. 1939 (P) Nickel Doubled Monticello DDR

DDR stands for Doubled Die Reverse, which refers to an error where the doubling occurs on the back side of the coin. This error results in a "double vision" effect, particularly noticeable on the words "Monticello" and "Five Cents" when viewed under a coin microscope or jeweler's loupe. Coins with this error are highly sought after by collectors. For example, an MS 67 coin was valued at $4,600 in 2002, and an MS 67+ reached $6,000 in 2023. Additionally, an MS 67 FS sold for $23,500 in 2019 but saw a decrease in value to $11,500 in 2023.

6. 1942 D Re-punched Mint Mark

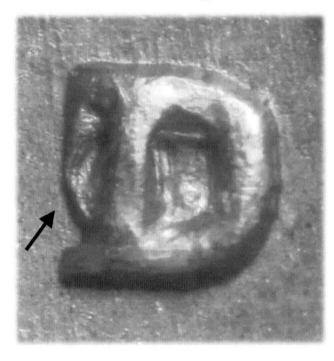

These coins feature a re-punched P, D, or S mint mark on the reverse side, with the most notable example being the 1942 D over horizontal D error, where the mint mark was struck twice at a 90-degree angle. These nickels are rare and valuable, with prices ranging from $135 to $5,750 depending on their condition. Coins with Full Steps are particularly sought after, with estimated values between $3,000 and $7,250.

One such coin set an auction record in 2013, selling for $15,275. However, the highest-priced example in the series was a Full Steps specimen, which fetched $32,200 in 2006. Another notable variety includes coins with a doubled P mint mark, with the most expensive being the 1942 P/P MS 66 Type 2 RPM nickel, sold for $1,050 in 2022.

7. 1942 Nickel Double Die Obverse

The DDO (Doubled Die Obverse) nickel error occurred when the die struck the coin's obverse two or three times during the minting process, leading to unique doubling on different parts of the design. While each error coin is distinct due to the varying locations of the doubling, they generally sell for a few hundred dollars. The most commonly known error is found on 1942 P nickels Type 1, where the date and the word LIBERTY show clear doubling. One of these error coins achieved a record auction price of $765 in 2018.

CHAPTER 11

Valuable Dime Errors

Are you thinking about adding Roosevelt dime errors to your collection? While many errors may seem minor and hold little value, certain ones can be incredibly valuable!

Roosevelt dimes have been minted in the billions since 1946, making them a staple in circulation but not necessarily a favorite among collectors due to their commonality.

However, it's worth reconsidering this coin. Roosevelt dimes with well-known errors can be worth far more than their face value.

Identifying these valuable errors can be challenging, which is why we've put together a list of the most sought-after dime errors. Whether you're looking to profit from your dimes or expand your collection, this list will provide useful insights.

Top Error Dimes Worth Money

1. 1982 No-Mintmark Strong Roosevelt Dime

The P mint mark was first introduced in 1980 to identify coins minted in Philadelphia. However, due to the manual process of adding mint marks, occasional errors occurred, such as omitting the mark altogether. This mistake happened with approximately 75,000 Roosevelt dimes struck in 1982, which were produced without a mint mark. The rarity of this error significantly boosts the value of these dimes.

There are two distinct varieties of the 1982 no-mint mark dime: one with a strong strike and another with a weaker strike. The dimes featuring a strong strike tend to be more valuable, with specimens graded MS65 potentially fetching prices up to $2,185.

2. 1965 Roosevelt Dime Broad Strike

During the minting of the 1965 Roosevelt dimes, occasional technical issues resulted in coins being struck without a fully formed rim, even though the obverse and reverse designs were unaffected. These error coins are notable and can command prices of around $80 for those graded at MS65.

3. 1969-D/D Dime RPM

RPM stands for re-punched mint mark, a term used to describe an error on older coins where the mint mark was manually stamped onto the die as one of the final steps. Occasionally, the mark would be misaligned, resulting in the earlier attempts being visible beneath the final mark. These errors are denoted as D/D or D over D. In 2019, two such coins—an MS 67 and an MS 64 FB—sold on eBay for $300 and $400, respectively.

4. 1968 Dime Doubled Die

This type of error happens when the dies strike the planchet multiple times, resulting in a doubled design on the coin. Although this error is relatively common among dimes, it still holds value. For instance, 1968 dimes exhibiting this doubling error can range in value from $65 to $160, depending on their condition.

5. 1968 No S Dime

Coins with this error are extremely rare. In 1968, the San Francisco Mint primarily produced proof dimes, most of which feature the "S" mint mark. However, a few unmarked examples exist, making them highly sought after.

The exact reason for the missing mint mark is unclear, though it's speculated that the error occurred during the transfer of the mint mark from the coin's reverse to its obverse.

Given the scarcity of the 1968 No S Roosevelt dimes, their value is significant. If you're looking to purchase one, you can expect to pay approximately:

- $12,000 for a PR 65 grade dime
- $13,500 for a PR 66 grade dime
- $16,800 for a PR 67 grade dime
- $20,000 for a PR 68 grade dime
- $38,000 for a PR 69 grade dime

6. 1999-D Roosevelt Dime Broad Struck on a Cent Planchet

The 1999-D Roosevelt dime is particularly notable for being broad-struck on a cent planchet, an error that seems almost impossible, making this coin extremely rare and unique. A cent planchet is larger than a dime planchet, so when the dime was struck on it, the design didn't fully cover the planchet, leading to a broad-strike error where the design extended beyond the collar.

This unusual error also resulted in a distinctive color mix due to the metal combination, with variations ranging from violet and blue-green to orange and gold. Only two such error coins are known to exist.

One of these rare dimes, graded MS65 by the Professional Coin Grading Service (PCGS), fetched $10,000 at auction, highlighting its significant value and rarity in the world of coin collecting.

7. 1970 Doubled Die Reverse Dime

Doubled die reverse errors are prevalent across various grades and in all three U.S. Mint facilities. This type of error occurs when parts or all of the coin's design, including portraits and inscriptions, appear doubled. The doubling results from the design being imprinted onto the master die at slightly different angles, leading to visible overlaps known as doubling.

These errors can occur on both the obverse and reverse sides of a coin. However, for the 1970 dime, many of the doubled die errors are found on the reverse. You may notice visible doubling or even triple overlaps in the inscriptions, particularly in the phrases "UNITED STATES OF AMERICA" and the denomination at the bottom of the coin.

The value of a 1970 doubled die reverse dime typically ranges from $20 to $30, but coins in mint condition can fetch up to $90.

8. 1975 S/S Proof Dime, Re-punched Mint Mark

In addition to the missing "S" mint mark error found on some 1975 proof dimes, there's another, less rare error known as the "S over S" variety. This error occurs when a second "S" mint mark is punched over the first one, which can be seen using a magnifying glass or loupe.

The value of a dime with this error largely depends on its condition. The Professional Coin Grading Service (PCGS) has certified five such examples in near-perfect PR69 condition with a deep cameo designation. Without the error, one of these coins would typically be worth about $16. However, with the "S over S" error, the value jumps significantly to around $800.

CHAPTER 12

Valuable Quarter Errors

Top Error Quarters Worth Money

1. 2000 D Virginia Quarter, Double Struck and Struck Off-Center

Sometimes, coins exhibit multiple errors simultaneously, as seen with a Virginia quarter struck at the Denver Mint in 2000. This particular coin wasn't ejected after the initial strike and received a second strike, which was also off-center. The result is a highly unusual appearance. Graded MS64 by the Professional Coin Grading Service (PCGS), this unique error coin fetched over $700 at auction.

2. 1983 Quarter Overstruck on an Amusement Token

It's hard to imagine how a 1983 quarter ended up being struck on an amusement token, but such coins do exist. The likelihood of this being purely accidental is incredibly slim, leading many to believe these coins were intentionally created. These unusual coins feature the recognizable design of an amusement token, with elements like lucky clovers and the phrase "THIS IS MY LUCKY DAY" over Washington's face on the obverse.

All known examples of this error come from the Philadelphia Mint, and they are the only coins of any denomination known to be struck on this particular type of token. In 2014, one collector purchased an example graded MS65 for an impressive $15,862.50.

3. 1983 P Spitting Eagle

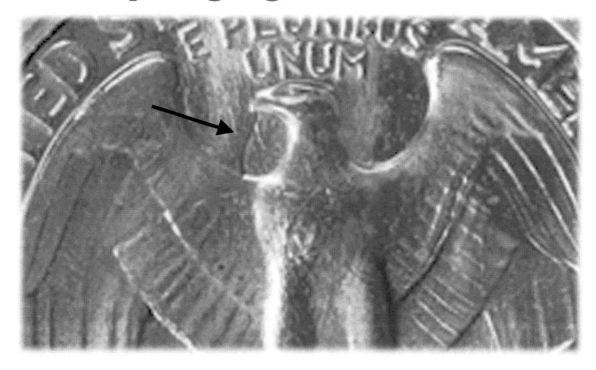

The "Spitting Eagle" is a well-known error associated with the 1983 quarters, recognized as one of the most prominent minting mistakes in this series. This error is caused by a die clash, where the dies strike each other without a planchet in between, resulting in a small line under the eagle's beak on the next coin produced.

These quarters were minted in Philadelphia, and both the PCGS and NGC acknowledge these 1983 quarters as a distinct variety. In circulated condition, these coins typically fetch about $1 or $2. However, those in mint state can range from $40 to $500, depending on their grade, with MS 63 to MS 66+ examples being the most sought after. The highest-known price for a Spitting Eagle quarter in MS 66+ grade was $504, achieved in 2018.

4. 1983 Quarter Struck on a Nickel Planchet

Occasionally, you might find a 1983 quarter that was mistakenly struck on a planchet meant for a nickel. Since a quarter is larger than a nickel, these error coins are lighter and exhibit missing parts of the design, resulting in a coin that is smaller than a regular quarter. The value for these unique error coins typically falls between $180 and $260.

5. 1976 D Quarter, Double Die Obverse

Double die errors happen when a die used to strike coins is mistakenly struck more than once with a hub, causing a slight shift between strikes. This creates a doubled image on the die, which is then transferred to the coins it strikes. Some bicentennial quarters minted in Denver in 1976 display a double die error on their obverse side, identified by the code FS-101.

This error can significantly increase the coin's value. Even coins in lower grades, like a grade 4, are valued at around $20 by PCGS. As the grade improves, so does the value, with coins graded 25 reaching into the three-figure range. An "extremely fine" XF45 example is worth approximately $235.

Coins in mint state are valued even higher—an MS60 grade coin is valued at around $725, while an MS65 can fetch up to $3,250. The finest known example of a 1976 Denver quarter with this error, graded MS66, sold at auction in 2023 for an impressive $8,400.

6. 2005 P Minnesota Extra Tree Quarter

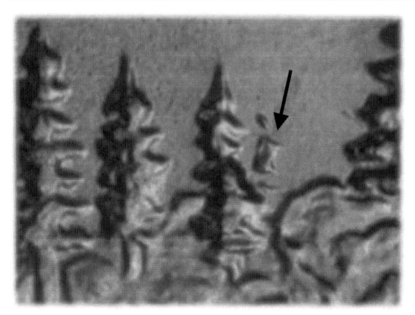

An error on one of the dies used to mint the 2005 P Minnesota quarter led to the creation of a variant known as the "Extra Tree." To spot this variant, you'll need to use a microscope or a loupe. Focus on the three trees located immediately to the right of the state outline on the coin. To the right of the third, smallest tree, you might notice a few small blobs resembling the tip of another tree—this is the "extra tree" feature.

The value of this error coin depends largely on how clearly the extra tree is visible and the overall condition of the coin. According to the Professional Coin Grading Service (PCGS), a coin with this error graded MS62 is valued at approximately $10, while one graded MS67 can be worth up to $90.

7. 2005 P Kansas Quarter, Missing Clad Layer on Reverse

Occasionally, the process of applying the cupronickel cladding to the copper core of a planchet encounters issues. This was the case with a 2005 Kansas quarter struck in Philadelphia, where the cladding was missing from the reverse side of the planchet. This quarter was later graded as AU 58 (About Uncirculated) by the grading agency ANACS and fetched $500 at auction.

8. 2004 D Wisconsin State Quarter: Extra Leaf Low

The Statehood Quarters Program is known for producing a limited number of coin varieties, making any error coins from this series especially valuable. Among the rare errors is the 2004 Wisconsin Extra Leaf Quarter, which comes in two varieties: the Low Leaf and High Leaf. These varieties feature an additional maize husk on the left side of the corn ear, with one husk positioned lower and the other higher, a detail absent from regular Wisconsin quarters.

This extra maize husk is considered a significant error, making the Wisconsin Extra Leaf Quarters some of the most notable minting errors in the entire Statehood Quarters series. In fact, a 2004 D Wisconsin Extra Leaf-Low Quarter, graded MS67, fetched an impressive $6,000 at auction in 2020.

9. 1966 Washington Quarter DDR

A doubled die reverse is an error that results in duplicated design elements on the surface of a coin, caused by misalignment during the minting process, either with the die or hub. The intensity of this doubling can vary from subtle, barely perceptible differences to more dramatic, easily noticeable effects.

Coins with prominent doubling are particularly sought after by collectors and often command a higher value. For example, a quarter with a doubled die reverse error, graded XF 45, set an auction record by selling for $920 in 2012.

10. Quarter Struck on a Dime Planchet

This error occurred when a quarter was mistakenly struck on a dime planchet, resulting in a coin with some design elements missing due to the smaller size of the dime planchet. Such an error coin can be quite valuable, with prices reaching up to $300.

11. 1943 Silver Quarter Double Die

A double die error occurs when the coin's design features overlap due to a misalignment during the die creation process. In the case of the 1943 quarter, this error is prominently found on the obverse side of the coin.

Among the 1943 Silver Quarters, there are notable examples of this error, with particularly prominent cases identified from both the Philadelphia and San Francisco mints.

The 1943 no-mint mark quarter with a double die error from Philadelphia is especially valuable. In circulated, extremely fine condition, it can be worth around $2,750. If the coin is uncirculated, its value increases significantly, reaching up to $5,500. For those in higher grades like MS 65, the price can soar to as much as $12,000.

On the other hand, the 1943 S quarter with a double die error, while still valuable, is not as highly prized. In extremely fine condition, it can be valued at $200. In uncirculated condition, with an MS 60 grade, the value can double to $550, and for an MS 65 grade, it can rise further to $1,650.

12. 1963 Washington Quarter DDO

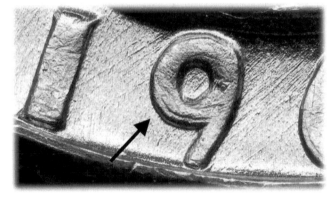 

This type of error occurs when the die shifts during the striking process, causing the design to land slightly off its intended position on the coin's surface. For instance, a Philadelphia quarter of this variety, graded MS 67+, achieved a record price of $1,680 in January 2022.

In contrast, a 1963 D MS 65 DDO Washington quarter fetched a lower price, selling for $552 at a Heritage Auctions event in April 2018.

13. 1963 Washington Quarter DDR

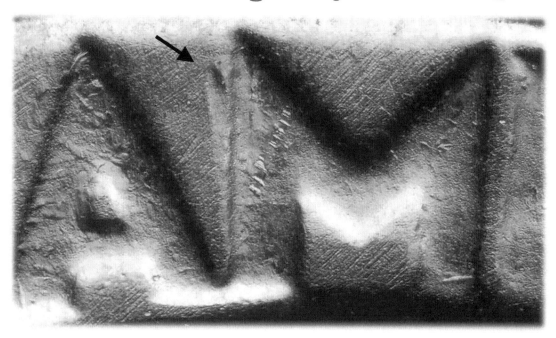

This error involves the doubling of letters or images on the reverse side of the coin. The most notable example is a 1963 MS 65 Washington quarter, which stands out as the highest-graded coin with this particular error. At an auction in 2018, a collector paid $720 for this rare and sought-after piece.

14. 1963 D Quarter Struck on a Silver Dime Planchet

This error occurs when a coin is mistakenly struck on the wrong type of planchet. For example, a 1963 D Washington quarter was minted on a planchet meant for a dime, resulting in noticeable traces of the precious metal on its surface. Additionally, these coins often feature incomplete rims due to the smaller size of the dime planchet. A specimen with an AU 55 grade recently fetched $675, highlighting the value and rarity of such errors.

15. 1963 D Quarter Struck on a Cent Planchet

These quarter coins were produced when a die mistakenly struck a penny planchet, resulting in noticeable differences in size and the absence of standard edge features. A particularly notable example is a 1963 D Washington quarter, with a brown tone and weighing only 0.1069 ounces (3.03 grams), which was sold for $1,300 due to its rarity and distinctive characteristics.

16. 1937 Silver Washington Quarter, Doubled Die Obverse

If you're searching for a 1937 no mint mark quarter in mint condition, prices can range from around $36 for an MS60 grade up to $500 for an MS67 grade. The top-tier MS68 coin can fetch as much as $25,000. However, if you come across one of these quarters with a doubled die obverse error, its value can significantly increase. This error, caused by a misalignment during the die's creation, is most noticeable on the phrase "IN GOD WE TRUST" and the date.

Even in lower grades, these error coins are valuable, with prices starting over $100. In mint state, expect to pay at least $2,000, with higher-grade examples reaching $6,500 or more. The finest known examples, three coins graded MS66, are valued at $26,000 each by the PCGS.

BONUS CHAPTER

You've journeyed through the essential strategies, insider tips, and expert knowledge I've shared so far. But, there's more—something that could set your coin collection apart from the rest. This bonus chapter is not just an additional piece of content; it's a treasure trove of advanced insights and techniques that can elevate your coin-collecting game to the next level.

Imagine discovering methods that only a select few seasoned collectors are privy to—methods that could unlock hidden values in your collection or give you an edge in the marketplace. What you're about to uncover is the culmination of years of expertise, distilled into actionable steps that can transform your collection from ordinary to extraordinary.

10 Websites for Coin Collectors and Enthusiasts

The internet is a fantastic resource for learning about coins and coin collecting. However, it's also a place where misinformation can easily spread. Below is a list of the top coin-related websites, carefully selected for their reliable and valuable content. These sites offer a range of information, from educational resources to current market trends, and are suitable for collectors at all levels.

The United States Mint

The United States Mint's official website is an excellent resource for learning about U.S. coins and purchasing them directly. The site is divided into sections focused on shopping, history and learning, and news. Here, you can explore the history of the Mint, discover how coins are made, and access valuable coin-collecting tips. Additionally, the site provides updates on new coin releases and other Mint-related news. **Scan the code below to access the sites.**

PCGS CoinFacts

PCGS CoinFacts is a comprehensive resource for U.S. coin enthusiasts, offering detailed information on virtually every U.S. coin ever minted. The site provides high-quality images, detailed specifications, and price guides, making it an essential tool for collectors who want to dive deep into the history and value of their coins. **Scan the code below to access the sites.**

Newman Numismatic Portal

Funded by renowned collector Eric P. Newman, this portal is a treasure trove of numismatic research. It offers access to nearly 100,000 digitized books and periodicals, as well as detailed bibliographies and auction records. Whether you're a beginner or an experienced numismatist, this site has something for everyone. **Scan the code below to access the sites.**

CoinNews.net

CoinNews.net is one of the top sites for staying updated on the latest in the coin-collecting world. The site covers a wide range of topics, including U.S. Mint news, world mints, bullion prices, and auction results. It also offers useful tools for collectors, such as inflation calculators and currency converters. **Scan the code below to access the sites.**

NGC World Price Guide

The NGC World Price Guide is a valuable resource for those interested in world coins. This fully searchable database offers coin values, images, and detailed specifications, covering world coins from 1600 to the present. **Scan the code below to access the sites.**

Heritage Auctions

As the world's largest numismatic auctioneer, Heritage Auctions offers a vast database of auction records, detailed descriptions, and realized prices. Whether you're buying or selling, this site is a valuable resource for anyone involved in the coin market. **Scan the code below to access the sites.**

GreatCollections

Founded by Ian Russell, GreatCollections is a user-friendly auction house that serves both beginner and advanced collectors. With low buyer's fees and professional images of all coins, it's an excellent platform for buying and selling coins online. **Scan the code below to access the sites.**

Mint Error News

Specializing in mint errors, this site offers a wealth of information for collectors interested in error coins. The downloadable Mint Error News Magazine is a highlight, featuring full-color pictures, recent discoveries, and educational content. **Scan the code below to access the sites.**

American Numismatic Association

The ANA's website is a hub for coin collectors, offering a wide range of resources, including a digital copy of The Numismatist magazine, virtual tours of the ANA Money Museum, and special tools for young collectors. **Scan the code below to access the sites.**

Kitco Bullion Prices

Kitco is a go-to resource for current and historical prices of precious metals, including gold, silver, platinum, palladium, and rhodium. It's particularly useful for those interested in the bullion value of their coins. **Scan the code below to access the sites.**

These websites represent some of the best resources for anyone interested in coin collecting, providing a mix of historical context, market data, and educational materials to help you build and maintain a valuable collection.

I hope you've found this bonus chapter valuable and that it has deepened your appreciation for the fascinating world of coin collecting. Your feedback is incredibly important to me, as it helps me continue to provide the best possible content for collectors like you. If you enjoyed this book or have suggestions for improvement, I would greatly appreciate it if you could take a moment to leave your honest review on Amazon. Your thoughts not only guide me but also help others in their coin-collecting journey. Thank you for your support and happy collecting!

CONCLUSION

As we reach the conclusion of this book, it's clear that the world of coin collecting is more than just a hobby—it's a journey through history, a treasure hunt, and an investment opportunity all rolled into one. The future of coin collecting looks bright, with emerging trends such as digital advancements in coin authentication and the growing popularity of error coins and rare varieties. The enduring appeal of coins lies not only in their historical significance but also in the personal stories and connections they create between collectors.

Coin collecting has stood the test of time, and it's poised to continue thriving for generations to come. Whether you're a seasoned numismatist or just beginning your collection, the possibilities are endless. The key to success lies in continuous learning, staying engaged with the numismatic community, and always keeping an eye out for the next treasure.

As you continue your journey, remember that this book is just the beginning. The resources provided will help you stay informed and connected, ensuring that your passion for coin collecting only grows stronger. Thank you for joining me on this exploration of the fascinating world of coins, and may your collection continue to bring you joy, knowledge, and perhaps even a little bit of fortune. Happy collecting!

Made in the USA
Middletown, DE
30 August 2024

60044186R00073